Ermiyas

1 800-423-7233   W.A oshA

1 800-423-7233

SENIOR CARE

CARE

BY

DESIGN

THE BETTER ALTERNATIVE
TO INSTITUTIONAL ASSISTED LIVING
AND MEMORY CARE

CHRISTIAN POTRA
with DR. STEPHEN MORRIS
and MICHAEL HEARL

MADE FOR
SUCCESS

Made for Success Publishing
P.O. Box 1775 Issaquah, WA 98027
www.MadeForSuccessPublishing.com

Distributed by Made for Success Publishing

First Printing

Library of Congress Cataloging-in-Publication data
Potra, Christian with Hearl, Michael and Morris, Dr. Stephen
SENIOR CARE BY DESIGN (in a Post-Covid Era): The Better Alternative to Institutional Assisted Living
p. cm.

LCCN: 2020947330
ISBN: 978-1-64146-649-3 (*Hardback*)
ISBN: 978-1-64146-535-9 (*Paperback*)
ISBN: 978-1-64146-576-2 (*eBook*)
ISBN: 978-1-64146-577-9 (*Audiobook*)

Printed in the United States of America

For further information contact Made for Success Publishing
+14255266480 or email service@madeforsuccess.net

TABLE OF CONTENTS

4. Do I Have What It Takes?

5. Is My Property Right For an AFH?

6. Operating a Senior Living Facility

7. Conclusion

FOREWORD

As a physician with specialties in emergency medicine and public health, I look at the situation of elder care in America from two vantage points: the individual and the system. I have first-hand knowledge of providing care to the elderly. From this perspective, I can attest that great improvement is needed in the senior care and housing industry. The institutional settings of the majority of long-term care facilities, and their largely for-profit financial structures, have produced a system that does not serve well the needs of its clients, the most vulnerable of our country's population.

Health care in the United States is in a state of rapid change. It is being reshaped by the COVID-19 pandemic, which has both exposed its weaknesses and prompted it to remarkable advancements. Vaccines for the virus have been developed and made available in record time. Approaches to critical care therapies have been refined to keep more patients alive. There have been recent breakthroughs, most in process before the pandemic, for treatments such as immunotherapy, technology making virtual visits possible through telehealth, and advances in record-keeping and communications. But, inadequacies and failures in early detection through testing and widespread implementation of infection control measures have taken a deadly toll. Those who have suffered the most are the elderly.

The processes of health care are in constant flux, and structures for both delivering care and paying for it are unfathomably complex. The insurance industry is multi-layered, duplicative, and often leaves uncovered those least able to pay themselves. Our rapidly growing older population is adding pressure to an already strained system. Even those familiar with the system often have difficulty navigating its complexities. Consider how daunting it must be for families and elders trying to understand and make decisions about meeting their increasing health care needs.

Decision-making in such complex situations involves making judgments and balancing priorities across very different arenas. The immediate focus may be on medical needs, insurance coverage, pharmacy, or rehabilitation. It's almost impossible to think about finance and insurance and housing and illness all in the same moment. How do you do a cost-benefit analysis when one of the factors is emotional wellbeing? When there are so many unknowns?

Decisions about senior care require a clear understanding of the options. The type of long-term care setting chosen will affect interface with health care and other services, and the outcomes this has for wellbeing. This setting also largely determines the senior's quality of life, which has a well-known impact on health status. Where seniors live, their circumstances, and the process of deciding on assisted living options all have significant influences on quality of life. For most seniors, independence and autonomy are of particular importance. The extent that these principles are supported in a facility should guide decision-making. Other important considerations are safety, cost, convenience, and personal preferences. Consistency of care and family support are extremely important. Taking time for this decision is basic to making good choices that will impact the whole family.

To make good decisions about these options, you need to start the process in advance of an emergency need. Many families are thrown into crisis by a sudden necessity to place parents or relatives in assisted living. Far better to begin this exploration earlier in the process, so suitable options can be worked out in advance. We have an obligation to assist elder family members with a system that is not user-friendly, and that often puts the bottom line before the welfare of those it is intended to serve—the patients.

Working in emergency medicine, I'm aware of the numerous specialties involved and the unique features of various emergencies. With my public health hat, I understand the complexity of the system with its millions of moving pieces. Overall, I appreciate the hard work of thousands of clinicians and support staff. Defects built into the system push many facilities to this focus on the bottom line as the way to keep their doors open. When they stay open, they continue to serve their communities; a hospital or clinic fails everyone when it closes its doors. It's important for me to express belief in good intentions. Few go into health care without them. Call me naïve, but I believe almost everyone from insurance executives to medical providers to the hospital cleaning staff has the patient's wellbeing in mind. People will do the right thing, given the opportunity, understanding, and means to do so.

Taking this perspective will help you navigate the health care maze by utilizing the human support that is available. People will help when they can, and when they tell you they cannot help, take them at their word. Move on, for it is the time to think of an alternative solution. From my experience, an attractive alternative solution is offered by adult family homes. These are homes in residential neighborhoods that have been converted to provide daily living needs and other care services to a small number of elders, generally up to six or eight per home. The smaller staff and home-like setting lead to more personalized care and response to individual preferences. Risks of exposure to infection or miscommunications around medical and health needs are lower. The family often lives nearby, and the community may be familiar.

Regardless of what option you are considering, reading this book is a step forward. Many of the diverse elements of senior care and housing, including finances, housing, family relations, and health care, are discussed. At times the connection of these elements is not particularly obvious, such as getting food the elder likes and being given support to thrive, rather than slip into depression. Or, the connection can be clear, such as the elder getting appropriate triage based on sound knowledge, data, and communication when illness occurs, or being sent inappropriately to the emergency room with almost no information.

I believe in the importance of considering health implications in all decisions about senior care. Overall, I do not believe our health care system is doing a good job of taking care of our elderly. That is my motivation for collaborating on this book with the team from MyAFH, Chris Potra and Mike Hearl. Focusing on long-term care for the elderly, this book gives me a chance to highlight the more attainable opportunities elders can take to improve health, and the precautions families can observe to ensure elders' wellbeing and safety.

In the chapters of this book, my role is to address some of the health care challenges facing our aging population. Often I do this through scenarios depicting what happens when elders interface with emergency and medical care, from a good versus bad outcome viewpoint. There are solutions offered in the book, which can be summarized as the concept that individualized care and personal service are better than institutional systems. When being with your family is not an option, being with people who know you and care for you is far superior to being with strangers.

Working together, Chris, Mike, and I intend for this book to provide you with the foundation and tools you need to make the best possible decision about long-term care for yourself and your family.

—*Stephen Morris, MD, MPH*

INTRODUCTION

CARING FOR THE elderly has become a major issue in America. Most American families at some point must deal with aging members whose needs for care are beyond what the family can provide. When it becomes clear that parents or relatives can no longer live at home without such assistance or memory care, the family faces decisions that are often complicated and difficult. The options for senior care are unfamiliar to most, and have changed significantly in the last several years. Although the image of nursing homes and large assisted living/memory care facilities usually comes to mind, new senior care options such as adult family homes are increasing. These small homes with eight or fewer elders are located in residential neighborhoods, and offer a home-like setting while providing needed care.

This book provides information and assistance in exploring the option of adult family homes for senior care. These are also called adult residential care, group homes, and board and care homes. The many advantages of this type of elder living situation will be fully described. The process of evaluating both personal and family considerations in selecting an adult family home and the process of assessing them as a business opportunity are also included in detail.

To give perspective, here is some background on elder care in America. Changes in family structure, lifestyles, and economics since the mid-1900s created an industry to provide elder care. Many American families were no longer able—or willing—to manage the day-to-day care needs of aging parents or relatives who were increasingly frail or ill. Historically, societies have had poorhouses and old folks homes. The United States characteristically turned these charitable facilities into a vast capitalistic enterprise.

The senior care and housing industry emerged in the 1950s and 1960s as nursing homes where elders received meals, housing, and assistance with daily living needs. These were called many names: nursing homes, assisted living facilities, skilled nursing facilities, nursing facilities, custodial care facilities, long-term care facilities. Their size varied from a few residents, such as 10 to 12, to large institutions housing more than 200 residents. The industry was further shaped by a series of laws.

- Social Security in 1935 set the stage for the private enterprise model in the U.S. In an attempt to keep elders out of public poor houses, the act prohibited payments to residents of public institutions. That sparked the rise of private nursing homes.

- The Hill-Burton Act of 1954, primarily meant to fund hospitals, was expanded to offer loans and grants to build nursing homes that agreed to provide low-cost care. This instituted the medical model of nursing homes that housed elders in institutions that resembled hospitals more than an apartment or multi-family home. This model is still prevalent today.

- Medicare and Medicaid in 1965 put a major infusion of money into the industry. Medicare, the federal health insurance program for people over 65, was set up to pay for doctor and hospital visits (later, medications and other therapies were added). Medicare had provisions to pay for short-term stays in convalescent homes, meant to assist elders to recover from acute illness or injury. Medicaid covered medical care for the poor.

Many nursing homes capitalized on Medicare by adapting to provide higher-level convalescent care services, intermingling these skilled nursing care beds with residential long-term care beds. This caused a blurring of distinction between nursing homes and skilled nursing facilities. By offering skilled nursing care services to some residents, nursing homes could significantly augment their income. The caveat was that Medicare would only pay for 100 days (recently expanded to 120 days) following a medically necessary 3-day hospitalization. After that, the elder either had to find another form of payment or leave the facility.

Medicaid is funded by matching state and federal funds, and coverage varies significantly from state to state. Through Medicaid, the U.S. and state governments use taxpayer money as the de facto payer for a large percentage of nursing home residents, currently over 75% of total resident days. The level of payment, however, does not cover expenses in long-term care facilities, creating serious problems with quality of care.

Before the late 1960s, nursing home care was relatively inexpensive. In addition, few people lived long enough to require much, if any, time in long-term care. Burgeoning health care costs and the rapidly rising elderly population changed this picture. In the nearly 100 years from 1960 to 2050, the population of those 85+ has rocketed an amazing 900%, rising from less than 0.5% to 4.5% of the total U.S. population.[1]

The majority of elders (73%) are still cared for in home settings in America. But the large numbers residing in America's nearly 30,000 long-term care facilities, estimated to be about one million people, often face living conditions that are far below optimal. The funding structures for long-term care often lead to payments that fail to cover expenses. As a result, there has been widespread substandard care and cutting corners to improve the corporate bottom line. Add to that insufficient government regulation and failure of industry oversight structure, compounding over 85 years. These factors produced a crisis of confidence in the long-term care industry in the early 2000s with scandals involving elder abuse and neglect as well as financial exploitation and Medicare fraud.[2]

There had to be a better way. This flawed business model of mostly private enterprise senior care and housing created pressure for change in response to society's need. During the 1990s, a different model began to coalesce that promised more personalized, home-like settings for quality and compassionate elder care. It was innovation in an industry changing with time and demands for a better structure for elder care. The adult family home model was the result. Regulations were enacted, mostly at the state level, to license homes in residential areas to provide care for limited numbers of seniors, between 1 and 8 residents. Although regulations vary by state, they generally cover structures and safety of the house and grounds, care standards for residents, and training requirements for personnel and business owners.

This new model for senior care and housing has many advantages: The settings are home-like, the numbers of residents and staff fewer, staff turnover is less, operators and caregivers know residents personally, homes are in neighborhoods that may be close to the elder's family and in a familiar community. Elders may be able to live in a home with others of shared backgrounds. These adult family homes can provide higher levels of care as needed, without seniors having to move between facilities. Personal preferences of seniors can be honored in this more intimate, smaller setting. By having small numbers and stable personnel, these homes reduce the risks of infection. This book describes these benefits in more detail, both from the perspective of families seeking a better placement for loved ones who cannot remain at home, and from the view of people looking for investment and business opportunities in a humane and responsible segment of the senior care and housing industry.

The impact of the COVID-19 pandemic on the nursing care industry has starkly exposed its many flaws. According to the American Association of Retired Persons, this has been "an American tragedy" during which an inordinate number of deaths have occurred in long-term care facilities:

"In one of the most devastating health debacles in our nation's history, some 54,000 residents and workers in long-term care facilities died of causes related to the coronavirus within four months of the first known infection . . . Fewer than 1% of Americans live in long-term care facilities. But 40% of COVID-19 deaths have occurred there."[3]

The flawed structure of the nursing home industry was utterly incapable of meeting the crisis brought on by the COVID-19 pandemic. By the close of 2020, the death toll in long-term care facilities had surpassed 94,000, with over 300,000 infected staff and residents. With nursing homes the default choice for elder Americans needing assisted living care, placing large numbers of susceptible elders in big institutional settings with multiple staff exposure and poor quality of care, the stage was set for the ravages of the pandemic. Fault must also be placed on government officials who failed to respond vigorously to the pandemic early on, made decisions that deprioritized nursing homes, and failed to implement early and widespread testing. Lack of inspections—most were suspended after the pandemic was underway—and unrestricted government cash infusion meant there was no accountability. Agencies, facility owners, and government officials all pointed at each other to take blame.

Many long-term care facilities were understaffed and under-funded prior to the pandemic. There were numerous citations for infection control deficiencies. The for-profit structure had reduced care quality at many homes, especially in the 10% owned by private equity investment groups. Their main reason for being in the nursing home business is to extract money through management contracts and lease agreements, legally removing money while cost-cutting to increase apparent value and sell at a profit. Every dollar squeezed out of nursing homes is not going to enhance care of its residents.[4]

Solutions to this situation are not coming soon. Politicians as well as industry businesses and insurers are not eager for reform and change. The COVID-19 crisis has highlighted the need for major changes to long-term care, but partnerships among all interested parties will take time to create.

Adult family homes (AFHs) offer an immediate solution. These options for senior care and living already exist in most states and are growing rapidly. As more people recognize the advantages AFHs offer to residents, staff, and owners, there will surely be increasing movement into this sector of long-term care. This book will provide the foundations on which to learn, evaluate, and plan whether involvement with an adult family home is in the future for you and your family.

1

GETTING THE LAY
OF THE LAND

*"The wise man looks down the road, and if he sees danger coming,
he steps around it: the fool just keeps going forward
on the same path and suffers for it."*
—King Solomon

*"The true measure of any society can be found
in how it treats its most vulnerable members."*
—Mahatma Gandhi

As MENTIONED IN THE FOREWORD to this book, clarity of vision can be a real game-changer. The better you can see important details, whether in sports, business, relationships, or in those challenging events that life has a nasty habit of throwing at us, the better off you'll be. In this book, we will explore that particular scenario where assisted living/memory care decisions loom, either for your own household or your parent's. Being able to look down the road at what is coming will be of great value for all parties concerned.

The benefit of looking forward, in terms of well-planned elder care, comes from making the right decisions at the right times. It allows early decision-making and puts you in a position to act on those decisions. Vision comes first, then intention, and finally, the means to act. Gaining this clarity of vision is what you can expect from the time you will invest in reading and digesting the material presented in this book. You will learn from knowledgeable and experienced people how to navigate this territory called "assisted living" and design your own unique vision, intention, and means.

> The terms "elderly" and "elder" do not have legal definitions. Such terms often have emotional significance for the people they include. For purposes of this book, the terms are used to mean people past middle age who have increased needs for assistive services.
> —Dr. Morris

> Many of the problems seen in the emergency department arise because families have failed to communicate about elder care issues, needs, and preferences. They have failed to plan, which results in their options being limited and more expensive at the time of crisis.
> —Dr. Morris

This chapter will help you get a "lay of the land" by orienting you in three basic areas associated with the assisted living industry: the facts, the finances, and the facilities. These are the foundations of this book.

The Facts

Too many people in their mid-life years find themselves facing a crisis with their aging parents. Just when mid-life adults are enjoying a comfortable lifestyle and have attained success in careers, sent children off to college, and are able to afford nice vacations, their equilibrium is shattered. One or both of their parents have reached the point where it's no longer possible to remain in their present home. Elderly parents may have serious health conditions, become disabled, or may be experiencing memory or cognitive issues that prevent them from managing their own lives safely. It's possible that parents are hiding information or covering for each other when it comes to the true condition of their health or mental status. They are embarrassed to share this information and don't want their children to see their changing abilities.

Typically, the adult children must step in and handle a crisis. The forces at work leading to the crisis may have been building for some time, but everyone wanted to avoid talking about these difficult life events. Elders and families are often in denial about the changing abilities of the elders or the gravity of the situation. The elderly parents themselves may not have insight into their limitations and increasing needs, and can be resistant to engage in discussion of such life-altering issues. There can be disagreement among adult children over what is the best course to take. Most people are confused about the choices available regarding continuing care for elders who cannot care for themselves.

> Elders may be reluctant to appreciate that they need assistance, to ask for help. It becomes the task of family members to gently and respectfully advocate for a safe situation that meets both the needs and preferences of their family member.
> —Dr. Morris

This is a growing issue because so many adults, mostly Baby Boomers, have reached middle age and are facing the needs of parents or relatives moving into old age. Today, there are about 76 million Baby Boomers in the U.S. That means that

10,000 Boomers will be turning 65 years old every day.[1] So, there is a wave coming down the road. But add to that the even more telling issue of the increase in the very old population, those 85 years plus. This group is expected to rise over the next 20 years from 6.5 million to 14.4 million, an increase of 123% just at the time boomers themselves will be moving into assisted living scenarios. If we look at the last 100 years, we see a 900% increase (from < 0.5% to 4.5%) in the number of people over the age of 85.

INCREASE IN 85+ U.S. POPULATION (1960-2050)

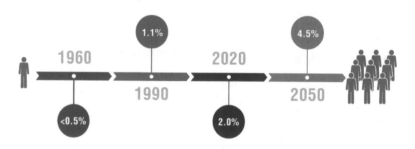

Figure 1

Increase in Very Old U.S. Population 1960 – 2050
Before 1940 the oldest old group was 75+
From 1940-1985 oldest old group was 85+
Based on data from U.S. Census Office, www.census.gov

The residential demand that these demographics represent will far outstrip current and projected availability. What is more, the levels of care that are needed will also increase, along with longevity. Today, 20% of those 85 and over need help with personal daily living activities. And 50% of those who reach 85 need to cope with various levels of diminished mental acuity and/or dementia.[2]

Just living long enough will eventually require some type of assistance with daily life needs. For most people, this means family members must assume responsibility. Those without relatives able or willing to provide this care must rely on institutional assistance. While some elders over age 65 continue living with family members, around 28% live alone. That is more than 14 million people! Since women live longer, almost half of women over 75 live alone. But, reaching 85-90 and beyond generally means that someone will need to provide assistance with activities of daily living.

Bottom line: what these statistics tell us is that the "perfect storm" is currently brewing with regard to assisted living senior care. There are more elderly people, in need of higher levels of care, which will demand more financial resources. And, as population statistics have shown, a lot of this burden falls on Baby Boomer households just as they themselves are having to deal with their own issues of aging.

Added to the above mix are the vulnerabilities and concerns with assisted living that the COVID-19 pandemic has exposed. It is reasonable to assume that the future will bring new problems with regard to health care needs and the complexity of the health care system. The current elder care system is not designed to accommodate changes demanded by the COVID-19 pandemic. Recent events have placed a spotlight on the vulnerability of the senior housing and care industry. There were avoidable tragedies related to natural disasters such as hurricanes Katrina and others. This demonstrated that many assisted living facilities did not have the capacity or the resources to respond to such crises. Their poorly executed disaster plans contributed to loss of life. In retrospect, such facilities appear to have been managed at the bare minimum of allowable standards. The same holds true for responses to containing and managing the spread of coronavirus infections in long-term care and assisted living facilities. Coronavirus has disproportionately affected nursing home residents and staff; more than 40% of deaths have occurred in those facilities.[3]

The Finances

Another serious consideration in caring for elders is the lack of financial resources. As most people retire and grow older, their income declines. In 2018, 9.7% of older adults were below the poverty level—over 5.14 million people. However, this percentage increased to 13.6% when adjusted for out-of-pocket medical expenses and other factors. The median income for older men was $34,267, while it was only $20,431 for older women.[4]

Sadly, many people fail to plan sufficiently for their retirement years, and either never set up an adequate retirement plan or run out of money in the plans they do have. Medical expenses are another significant reason for poverty and homelessness among elderly. As people age, their risk for disease and injury increases, while their medical insurance coverage generally declines. Specifically, when they need the most coverage because of their increasing medical needs, their insurance wanes and provides less coverage. Huge medical bills drain away savings and can force impossible choices between paying bills, buying medicines, and getting groceries.

This chart compares costs for different aspects of senior living and care in four types of facility settings: In Home Care, Memory Care, Adult Family Homes, and Assisted Living.

COST OF CARE

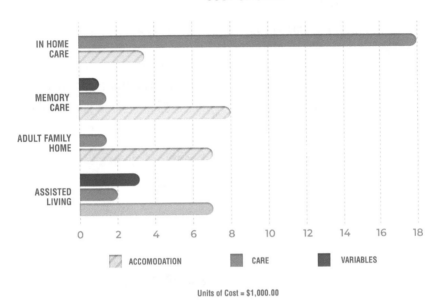

Units of Cost = $1,000.00

Accommodations: Cost of lodging or housing.

- In Home Care cost is an average $2,500 mortgage payment.

- Memory Care accommodations are usually a shared room, cost $8,000.

- Adult Family Home averages $7,000 for a private room.

- Assisted living is a shared suite for $7,000.

Basic Care: Basic assistance with living activities on a 24-hour basis.

- In Home Care is the average of 1 caregiver at $23/hour, 24 hours/day, 31 days/month.

- Memory Care and Assisted Living have varying packages that specify what is included.

- Adult Family Home adds an additional amount for more than the basic care.

Incidental Care Variables: Additional care items not in monthly contract.

- In Home Care and Adult Family Home have little or no additional costs because incidentals are included in the monthly rate.

- Memory Care and Assisted Living charge extra when care outside the monthly package is given.

The Facilities

The three main options for senior care—**Assisted Living/Memory Care Facilities, In Home Care, and Adult Family Homes**—will be covered in detail in future chapters. In order to get a picture of what these options look like, examples will be described that capture the essence of what families and elders experience.

NOTE: Many people confuse "nursing homes" with Skilled Nursing Facilities (SNF). The role of an SNF is not to provide long-term elder care, but to give professional medical care to people making a transition from an acute care hospital to another facility or back home. They offer rehabilitation and skilled nursing/medical services when patients are recovering from strokes, surgery, or acute illness and need such things as physical and occupational therapy, IV infusions, complex procedures, or medications that cannot be managed in assisted living facilities or at home. This type of facility is used when Mom or Dad have had hip replacement surgery or need therapy to regain function after a stroke. The goal is to get the patient healthy and back on the way to normal life.

Usually insurance has approximately 100- to 120-day limitations on stay in an SNF.

In Home Care remains the most frequent approach to managing elderly parents who are unable to live alone. U.S. Census Bureau statistics report that only around 5% of elders age 65+ live in some form of assisted living, including those called nursing homes, congregate care, assisted living, and board and care homes. But as seniors get older, the percent in such facilities increases. Around 25% of seniors 85+ and 50% of seniors 95+ live in some type of care facility. For many families, In Home care is a good option, at least for a while.

As the need for higher and higher levels of care develops, it means the elder will need to have caregivers in the home for increasing hours to provide more help with daily living activities. It's not uncommon for the hours caregivers need to be present in the home to increase from 4 to 8 hours, then to 12 or more hours per day. At current rates, generally $15-$30 per hour, that can cost from $5,400 to over $11,000 per month for 12 hours per day caregiving. Paying for home care workers to stay overnight, if needed, is usually a little less for those 12 hours.[5]

Assisted Living Facilities (ALF) make up the most common institutional option when an elder cannot remain at home, and family members are unable to take them into their houses for continuing care. There is a wide range of services and quality of care within this vast industry. At one end of the spectrum is the small neighborhood facility with 8-15 rooms for residents, who are provided around-the-clock support for activities of daily living. Medical and memory care typically are not included. Usually these facilities cost $6,000 - $8,000 per month. At the other end is an option called Continuing Care Retirement Communities (CCRC), also known as "life plan communities" that incorporate the entire continuum of aging care from independent living to medical, memory, and skilled nursing care. These are expensive, several-tiered large organizations that typically have a substantial entry fee, ranging from the low- to mid-six figures. Additionally, there are hefty monthly charges that can be well above $5,000 depending on the plan chosen. Very few people in the U.S. have the financial resources to take advantage of these "age in place" organizations.

Large Corporation Institutional Assisted Living

When most people think of nursing homes, they have in mind large institutions that resemble apartment complexes housing up to 100 or more seniors. Average size of these assisted living facilities across the U.S. is 33 beds per facility, with typical ranges being 25 – 120 beds. In 2020 there were 28,900 assisted living facilities in the U.S. with nearly one million licensed beds.[6] In Washington State, there are over 600 ALFs with around 30,000 beds.[7] A report in 2018 found 48,934 total licensed community residential beds in Washington State, but did not differentiate between Assisted Living Facilities and Adult Family Homes.[8]

Although many facilities provide care that is acceptable if not good, institutions that are larger give less personalized care. There is more staff turnover and less loyalty to employers and residents in these large institutions. Most institutions of this type in the industry are motivated by profit and not by relationships. Beds in corporate-run facilities are only valuable if filled; if a bed is empty or filled with a non-paying or low-paying resident, it is a significant loss. The cost of these facilities is often daunting; according to Genworth, a private, one-bedroom assisted living facility room is $40,000 to $50,000 per year in most states.

Moving from the family home, or from living in children's homes, is inevitably traumatic for elder people. When this move is into a large, impersonal assisted living facility, the trauma is multiplied. The resident is placed in a small, unfamiliar room with only a few personal possessions. If they are fortunate, they may be able to bring their beloved pet. Now, they must rely on strangers to provide for their needs—everything from meals to dressing and hygiene to housekeeping. Unless their room has a tiny kitchenette, the elder cannot even get a cup of tea without depending on a staff member. The number and training of staff also is a key measure of the quality of the living situation. With high resident-to-staff ratios, the large corporate ALFs do not have enough caregivers to respond quickly to elders' needs.

Some elders adjust well to living in large facilities, make new friends, and share activities, and seem satisfied with the care given. Others never fully bounce back from the disruption of leaving their familiar home and moving into a vastly different environment. Some slip into a downward spiral that leaves them worse off, slowly deteriorating mentally and physically. ALFs vary in the extent of services each provides, and one all-too-common scenario is the resident whose care needs have outstripped what the facility can manage. This situation of being "evicted" from the ALF places additional financial and emotional stresses on the elder and family.

Here is a recurring scenario for elders placed in large assisted living facilities:

Mom or Dad can no longer live by themselves, or require more care than family members can manage and need to be placed in an ALF that seems the perfect place. The transition goes smoothly, and the elder is getting all their needs met, giving the family peace of mind that they are safe and well cared for. For some time, things go well, and the elder enjoys the amenities and friendship in the facility.

As aging progresses and the elder needs more physical care, the family knows they must move up from the basic care package and planned in advance so they are able to afford the increased fees.

But, if the elder develops dementia, another entire level of care is needed. Approximately 5-8% of people over age 65 have some form of dementia, most frequently, Alzheimer's disease. This number doubles every five years after that. Memory issues affect 50% of seniors over 85 years old.[9]

In this example the dementia is mild at first and the facility continues to manage things, but as the disease progresses, the elder becomes increasingly difficult to contain, is prone to wandering, and gets combative toward staff. At this point, the facility decides it can no longer manage the necessary care and gives the family an "eviction" notice informing them they must move their elder within a week or two.

Families with enough money and resources can handle this by finding a memory care facility, but for many, it's an overwhelming challenge. If they face the problem of having used up their available resources, they are at the mercy of available government-supported care. In many situations, a social worker or discharge nurse is assigned to help the family figure out a plan. This usually involves discussion and provision of material describing facilities based on what the limited funds will allow. The family is responsible for researching and performing the vetting process. In many situations, the optimum facilities are full. Given the importance of timing, the family's hand is forced, and they struggle to make the best decision, too often with insufficient and or difficult to interpret information and inadequate guidance. If they must get Mom or Dad qualified for Medicaid (federal and/or state public assistance for health care), their options shrink even more. There are limited numbers of Medicaid beds in any given facility, and the nicer elder care facilities do not have any beds at all, as they only work with private pay residents. In some instances when there is a loyal, established relationship, a facility may have a policy allowing a resident to stay on after a predetermined amount of time and be converted into a Medicaid resident. There are requirements to qualify for Medicaid, including spending down assets to certain levels and properly filling out a new Medicaid application every year to stay in the program. Navigating through this complex, bureaucratic government system takes persistence and time.

Repeated moves for elderly people, particularly those with memory issues, is a traumatic and confusing experience. Those who experience serious illnesses, such as strokes or heart attacks, will be shifted from ALF into a skilled nursing facility after acute hospitalization. They spend weeks or months in rehabilitation, only to return to the same or a different ALF. Each change means relating to new caregivers and contending with a new environment. It can be too much for many elders, who decline quickly and have their lives shortened.

The best advice for families looking for senior care is to learn about the choices and costs, know the realistic

Most people have taken vacations that were chaotic, disappointing, and unsatisfying. In retrospect, they see that failure to plan led to the vacation's poor outcome. Big decisions in life are also impacted by failure to plan. Where your loved one goes when they need help with daily living is a big decision. Take time to plan ahead and avoid chaotic results. Prioritize the emotional wellbeing of your loved one above almost all other considerations. Ask yourself if this choice would be the one they would make for themselves.

—Dr. Morris

options for their situation, and have a plan—which requires making decisions before the crisis. Too many families let this situation creep up on them and face serious decision-making while dealing with Mom or Dad's crisis. But all is not gloom. There are options for long-term senior care that include comfortable, home-style living and are not financially impossible.

Adult Family Homes (AFH's) are a relatively new and rapidly growing option in elder care. These are residential homes that have been converted to meet requirements for senior care of up to 6-8 residents. Each resident has a room and receives help with activities of daily living by a trained caregiver. There is an operator who has the opportunity to also be the home's owner, often living in a separate area of the house around the clock. When needs for medical and skilled nursing care arise, these can usually be given within the home, without moving the resident. Most homes also include memory care. Costs for a room are typically around $4,000 - $6,000 per month. The average cost of assisted living in the U.S. is $3,750 per month; in Washington State, it is $4,625 per month.[10]

When elders are the family members of the owner/operator who has entered the business of running an Adult Family Home, costs can be minimal. This occurs when care for Mom or Dad is essentially paid for by income from other AFH residents, which is why some call it "zero cost senior care." Adult Family Homes offer the one pathway that brings together the potential for providing the best care possible along with better stewardship of family and estate finances. This high level of care is due to the favorable caregiver-to-resident ratio in Adult Family Homes, which is typically one staff to six residents. In Assisted Living Facilities, this ratio is often one staff to twelve residents or greater. More on this in a later chapter.

The Families: Adult Family Homes Solve Many Issues

Adult Family Homes constitute a growing segment of the senior care industry. In Washington State, there are about 3,200 AFHs with over 19,000 beds.[11] Many families are discovering the advantages of placing their mom or dad in an AFH. These small senior residences keep elders in a familiar community, offer a home-style atmosphere, low resident-to-staff ratios, personalized care, and flexibility as the elder's care needs increase. AFHs are regulated differently than Assisted Living Facilities, accept Medicaid residents, and tend to have residents who need higher care levels.

Here are three positive real-life examples of families' experiences with AFHs.

Example 1: Paula and Cory

Washington state couple Paula and Cory come from a family with a tradition of taking care of their elders. Alice, Paula's mother, lived in the 4-bedroom family home for over 50 years and raised 10 children. Paula and Cory had moved back into the family home with three of their children and built an addition on the property. Alice lived in the front part of the house and sold it to Paula with an agreement that she could remain there for the rest of her life. As Alice aged, the responsibility for figuring out what to do fell on Paula's shoulders. Exploring a suitable place for her mother to live out the last third of life brought up many difficult questions: would she be happy in a new place, would it be far away, was there enough money, would it impact her health negatively? Paula was exploring assisted living facilities and in-home care, not to mention juggling the life-altering decision of selling the family home.

Paula and Cory also owned a rental house that caused constant problems, and between expenses for both houses, they never seemed to get ahead. They were spending $2,500 in expenses monthly and not breaking even with rent. The renters were not reliable in keeping up the house and yard. With so many decisions crashing down on her, Paula was overwhelmed and frantic.

Several family members were in the medical field and knowledge-able about the senior care industry. Another one of Alice's daughters had connections with the owner of an AFH organization that operates, advises, and provides support for Adult Family Homes. Discussions began about converting the family home into an AFH. Initially, Paula and Cory thought it sounded too good to be true— that they could provide senior living for Paula's mom where she had a separate space from the other residents, and create a good income at the same time. They kept asking, "What's the catch?" They worried about financing and marketability, doubting anyone would pay as much as $4,000 per month to house their elderly parent in an AFH. They needed time to process what this could mean for their own and the children's futures.

Suddenly, there was a fire in the family home, causing Alice severe distress and creating more uncertainty about what to do. Paula urged her to continue discussions about converting the house to an AFH. The family learned they could get assistance to finance repairs and remodels to convert their home, turning it into housing for up to six adults. In addition, they could add an accessory dwelling unit (ADU), a separate 1,000 square foot, one-bedroom apartment for Alice while the main home was converted. For the AFH business, the grounds would be upgraded to meet standards and all safety requirements put in place. An additional incentive was that the AFH management company would rent the newly converted

AFH from the family and operate the business, taking care of all the regulations for getting it going.

Paula and Cory breathed a sigh of relief, as it was a challenge to meet over 700 requirements in their state for adult family homes. The company took care of the permitting, approvals, inspections, construction, and afterward operated the business and managed rentals, staff, insurance, and maintenance. It took a huge load off Paula, who could now run her own business while benefitting from a positive cash flow. Her mom had a nice apartment and, when needed, would move into one of the AFH rooms to receive higher levels of care. Alice was able to stay in the same house where Paula grew up, keep her same doctors, go to her same favorite grocery store and coffee shop, walk the same neighborhood and say "hi" to the same people.

Paula's mom is thriving at 84 years old and will never go to a nursing home. Now Paula and Cory know that they have a place to live when they get older, without having to worry about mortgage payments or running the business, all while making an income! They will not become a burden to their own children. Turning their family house into an Adult Family Home solved many issues for Paula and Cory, and partnering with a management company made the conversion process smooth. This turned a negative cash flow scenario into a nice profit while ensuring a pleasant, comfortable home setting to provide assisted living care for their aging mother. The value of their family home, now converted into an AFH, has increased from $365,000 before the fire to around $1.35 million.

The example of Paula and Cory provides one unique example, and every family's situation will be different. There are many options to consider and decisions to make. There is, however, an important factor to keep in mind; the concept of being a "good steward" with the resources entrusted into your hands. In this area, the model of the Adult Family Home shines particularly brightly. Investing in an

Adult Family Home, both short and long term, can mean the difference between severely depleting a family's finances and reducing their hard-earned estate, and preserving these for future generations.

One of the main reasons this book was undertaken is to encourage families to be good stewards, even when facing the challenges of providing assisted living choices. You can either spend down family resources or help them grow. With AFHs, you can realize the twin goals of attaining the best care for elders *and* carrying out wise stewardship.

Example 2: Ann and Charles

Ann was still working as a banker a few years ago when her husband Charles fell in the garage and hit his head. He was rushed to the emergency room, where they found blood clots in the brain that seriously affected his ability to function. He was given only a few months to live, and Ann knew he would need assisted living for the remainder of his life. This was devastating news for them, as an assisted living facility was not part of their plan.

Ann began doing research and looked at several facilities in the area, an arduous process that did not yield any good options. While driving to work, she noticed a sign for an Adult Family Home. She decided to investigate, since she knew very little about AFHs. Soon after she met with the owner, who answered every question she had, demonstrating years of experience caring for others. The AFHs mission was to show compassion and love to everyone in their home and provide the best and most personal care possible. The price was a concern to Ann, and she needed time to process how that would work for her family.

The doctors told her Charles would probably need assisted living care for only 3-4 weeks, as his prognosis was not good. Touched by the empathy and competence demonstrated at this AFH, Ann realized this was where her husband needed to be. She moved him in soon after, and those few weeks turned into three months, making the final phase of his life as happy and peaceful as possible. Ann was astounded at how staff at the facility took care of Charles, accommodating his needs and desires for the smallest things, from being served salmon every day to arranging transportation for his 90-year old mother to visit twice a week, brought from her assisted living facility, at no extra cost.

Looking back, Ann realizes this was the best decision she could have made. She has no regrets about the cost, saying the staff was incredible: "They took care of his needs, cooked his favorite meals, and brought in a hairstylist to take care of his hair and beard. It was first-class care day and night. . . Although my husband was only there for a few months, it was some of the best months he had . . . [it] renewed his faith in people and showed him that everyone matters, no matter the situation."

Example 3: Joe's Three Children

When Joe's three children discovered he was having trouble living alone in his apartment, his daughter Jane, who had medical power of attorney, brought him to live with her family in their home. He was diagnosed with dementia and became increasingly difficult to manage. Just as the other daughter Sally was about to move to another state, Jane shared that caring for their father was taking a toll on her and the family, and that she was at a breaking point. Jane had already changed her life to care for their dad, taking a leave from her job to keep up with the demands he presented 24/7.

Joe's dementia had progressed to the point that he no longer slept through the night. He would get up and wander outside in the middle of the night, and Jane wouldn't find out until the morning.

Joe was a smoker and that added to the worry about his safety. Jane was concerned that he would forget his lit cigar, creating a fire hazard that could hurt him and damage her home. He became destructive to things in Jane's home. Whenever she had to step out for a few moments to run errands or go shopping, she was anxious. She worried about what additional things would be broken, if Joe had fallen or wandered off, or if some major event happened while she was absent. Based on Joe's behaviors, he needed constant supervision for his safety and that of others. Jane simply could not provide that.

It was bad timing for Sally, who was on the verge of moving, but something had to be done to relieve Jane. Their brother was not as close to Joe and had little idea of how serious the problem was. He resisted moving their father at all, and the three siblings were having trouble coming to an agreement about what was best. Each had a different motivation and perspective. Finally, the sisters convinced their brother that Joe needed to be in a care facility, but knew it would be costly because of his wandering, disruptive behaviors.

Sally had financial power of attorney and explored AFH options for her dad. She called one weekend, and the owner of the AFH management company responded promptly. She was impressed that her call was returned over the weekend and immediately set up an assessment to decide the best placement for Joe. The AFH team took the three siblings for a tour of the available AFHs that could provide for their father's needs. The team mediated multiple conversations among all three children to help them reach an agreement. They recommended a home for Joe that was new construction, explaining it was in his best interest to be the first resident in the home so he could get the one-on-one attention he needed to make the adjustment. Later there would be five additional residents, and the caregivers would help Joe with that transition.

Every aspect of Joe's move was coordinated by the AFH team. It happened quickly to take the burden off Jane's shoulders, and Sally could move with peace of mind that her father was getting the care he needed. Joe's care was now handled by experienced caregivers, who provided necessary supervision, scheduled his doctor's appointments, and accompanied him for safety. Jane was able to repair her home and put energy into her family and job again. The three siblings were grateful for the spend-down Medicaid policy that helped them budget the cost of care, keeping Joe in the same home regardless of how much care he needed as his condition progressed. They were especially happy that their father was in a safe environment with caregivers trained in dealing with dementia and challenging behaviors.

Now Joe's three children can enjoy being with their father on his good days. They are also relieved of having to deal with overwhelming details of his care on the bad days. All feel very fortunate to have found an AFH for their father.

The Modern American Health System and Care for the Elderly

The intersection of the modern American health system and care for the elderly is often problematic. How elders are insured, who provides care, and barriers to optimum care are significant concerns. If you have engaged with this system, you understand that medical care for the elderly in America is challenging to obtain, inconsistent, and complicated. Medicare, the

> When elders use up benefits provided by Medicare and supplemental insurance, they face the "spend down" requirement for Medicaid (government assistance) and may lose whatever wealth their family has accrued.
> —Dr. Morris

primary insurance covering the over 65 population, and Medicaid which covers the poor and disabled, are extremely complex with minute rules about qualifications and duration of care in assisted living situations. While supplemental insurance is available, it also is variable and may be costly.

Who Cares for the Elderly? Care for the elderly and those with disabilities have elements which are unique. Elderly patients often have special needs, such as physiological changes of aging, screening for age-related disease, and working with their families when they are unable to advocate for themselves. To provide the highest quality of health care, medical personnel need the tools, time, and training to respond to these needs.

Geriatrics is the field of medicine concerned with care of the elderly, largely a subspecialty of internal medicine. This specialty takes into account everything from bone density to medication tolerance, memory problems, and social issues of the elderly. Geriatricians generally do an excellent job, and patients and families love them. Other health care providers value them. However, there are not nearly enough geriatricians for the current population, and this gap will get worse when the elderly population expands, as highlighted above. The result is that patients not lucky enough to have a geriatrician are cared for by an internal medicine physician, or family medicine physician (or affiliated nurse practitioner or physician assistant). There are currently not enough of these clinicians either, and the gap for them is also increasing.

> Medicine has become fractioned into subspecialties. These clinicians may be at a disadvantage as they navigate the complexity of elderly patients' needs while also managing the needs of their specific medical niche.
> —Dr. Morris

Additionally, the fields of medicine encompassing outpatient (clinic) and inpatient (hospital) care continue to diverge. This is good since there are too many differences in the two settings for a single clinician to be an expert at both; spanning the requisite medical knowledge to the nuances of electronic medical records and how to bill for services. There are geriatricians who specialize in each setting, but far too few. Non-geriatrician inpatient clinicians must care for elderly, children, post-surgical, intensive care, and other types of patients in the hospital. The same holds true for many internal medicine and family medicine clinicians. In both settings, no matter how well-meaning, they do not have the time or training to provide the highest level of care.

Barriers to Medical Care for the Elderly. Add to this situation the current state of health care in America. Many hospitals are struggling financially, there is not enough primary care, emergency departments are over-crowded, there are long waits for elective surgeries, and other inadequacies. In most clinicians' offices, a few minutes with each patient are typical. For an elderly patient with five chronic illnesses, taking fifteen medications, and who is hard of hearing, it is impossible to provide optimum care in such a setting.

Specific barriers to care for the elderly include challenges of transportation, need for accompaniment, and capacity to understand medical decisions and directions, among others. There is huge variability in elder care facilities regarding the type and quality of health care provided and the competencies of staff. This inconsistency is seen from facility to facility, location to location, and in the licensing bodies from state to state. Some facilities have staff with no medical training whatsoever, while others have a physician present on site 24 hours per day. When residents of a facility do get ill, the decision about when to seek care, when to call for transportation, and where to take them is also not clear. Early decision making regarding medical needs, which is critical in the elderly, is often inadequate and results in delayed and suboptimum care. This could lead to poor outcomes with unnecessary mortality and morbidity.

Getting the best health care for elderly patients is challenging and takes effort and planning. When the family or another advocate is not present and engaged, it is easy for important issues to be overlooked, patient concerns to be ignored, and miscommunication to happen. The health care system is unlikely to change rapidly, so steps must be taken to make it work for you and your family. This requires putting in the time to talk over health issues with elders, understand and keep records of their medical problems, medications, surgeries, allergies, and health history. A critical part of managing elder medical care is completing forms to document their health care wishes, including medical power of attorney, advance directives, and preferences regarding life-sustaining treatments. These are necessary to ensure that your loved ones get appropriate care.

The Way Forward

This chapter has laid out a high-level look at the territory of assisted living in terms of getting familiar with the basic element involving facts, finances, facilities, and families. It has provided you with facts, statistics, definitions, and examined the state of elder care in America. Hopefully, it has aided you in considering the way forward from here. In the next chapter, the content will go more deeply into the things you need to know about the Senior Care and Housing Industry as you design your own unique roadmap. Great design is about uncovering key nuggets and connecting the dots on the roadmap that reflect your own family's unique situation. A well-developed design is invaluable in seeking out the best assisted living setting for your loved one.

TIME	ENERGY	RESOURCES	MONEY
Are you able to give copious amounts of time to this project?	Do you have abundant energy for long hours of work?	Do you have multiple contacts in various aspects of the AFH business?	Are your financial assets sufficient for necessary cash infusions?

In this process of learning about senior care options and designing your own roadmap that will take you to your goals, you will need to keep in mind the acronym "TERM": As you evaluate the best approach for your family, these four considerations will play key roles in shaping your decisions. These are covered in-depth in a later chapter. The following chapter will take a look at what you need to know about the Senior Care and Housing Industry to design your roadmap through the territory.

2

DESIGNING YOUR MAP THROUGH THE SENIOR CARE TERRITORY

ANYONE CONSIDERING THE options for senior care during the last third of life will benefit from an understanding of the current senior care industry. You can look ahead, educate yourself and plan, or be thrust into making ill-informed choices. Even worse, you can leave the task to others: your children, relatives, or perhaps strangers. Your family will not thank you if this huge responsibility falls to them. They will be equally unprepared for this and less able to gauge preferences, setting the situation up for failure. Regardless of who is making decisions on your behalf, it is unlikely that this will result in an optimum situation.

The best approach would be to create a design for moving into and through the final third of life. Approaching these decisions thoughtfully can guide you to create what can be called "a good life." This period needs forethought and preparation so your whole family can flourish—from the senior in question to generations ahead.

You can rest assured that you are meeting needs in a satisfying and respectful way, along with being a good financial steward. But, the opposite of a good life is also possible and often becomes the default if nothing is done. This could mean anything from housing that the senior does not like, to unsafe conditions, premature death, and generations of bankruptcy.

> The best approach? Design your way into and through this final third of life, creating an optimal living situation.
> —Dr. Morris

Of one thing we can be certain: What has been traditional senior care will not suffice in the coming years. Currently, there are not, and there will not be in the future, enough facilities to provide traditional senior care. The current state of the industry cannot support the numbers that are coming as the Baby Boomers enter the last third of life. In 2018, more than 15% of the U.S. population was comprised of older adults, and in 2020 that percentage rose to 16.9%—that's more than one in every 7-8 people. The population over age 65 is projected to rise steeply over the coming years. This is largely due to Baby Boomers crossing the 65-year threshold. The first round of Boomers, born in 1946, turned 65 in 2011. Simply follow the numbers to get a sense of the impact:

> Simply put: the more you learn now regarding all the players and dynamics involved in the senior care industry, the better decisions you will make and the smoother the path you'll travel.
> —Dr. Morris

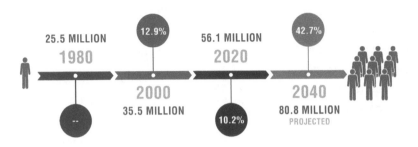

INCREASE IN 65+ U.S. POPULATION (1980-2040)

Year	US Pop over 65	% Total Pop	% Increase in Tot. Pop. 65+
1980	25.5 million	11.3%	--
1990	31 million	12.5%	21.5%
2000	35 million	12.4%	12.9%
2010	40.3 million	13.1%	15.1% (Boomers enter 2011)
2017	50.9 million	15.8%	26.3% (6 years of Boomers)
2020	56.1 million	16.9%	10.2% (3+years of Boomers)
2040	80.8 million	21.6%	42.7% (projected)
2060	95 million	22.0%	17.8% (projected)[11]

Of this group, racial and ethnic minorities increased from 23% in 2016 to a projected 28% in 2030. This is significant because health needs are greater for minorities, who tend to have more chronic disease and less access to medical care.[2]

According to research conducted by the U.S. Department of Health and Human Services, the number of "oldest-old" seniors is also increasing. Those 85 years and over are expected to more than double from 2016 to 2040—growing from 6.4 to 14.6 million, a whopping 129% increase. **That number could reach 18.9 million by 2050**.

To understand why this is so important, consider the impact of extended life expectancy. Seniors who reach age 65 have an average life expectancy of an additional 19.4 years (women 20.6 years, men 18 years). And, among seniors who reach age 65, about half (52%) will need some type of long-term care services during the rest of their lifetimes. The need for caregiving increases with age. When seniors reach the "young-old ages," 2% will need help with personal care, in the "middle-old ages" about 9% will need assistance with personal care and then that number hits 20% in the "oldest-old ages."[3] In other words, these elders cannot take care of their daily personal needs, such as bathing and dressing, cooking and eating, and household chores such as cleaning and laundry.

Healthcare concerns for the elderly change with age, so there is benefit to breaking the group up by age. This is the commonly used scale for categories within elderly:

- Young-old ages 65 to 74 years
- middle-old ages 75 to 84 years
- oldest-old ages ≥85 years
- oldest of the oldest-old ages >95 years

When seniors reach this stage in the last third of life (or sooner for those with disabling conditions), they require assistance with daily living activities. Many will be unable to continue living alone or at home with relatives. This is the point at which seniors and their families need to find an assisted living situation that will provide support for activities of daily living (ADLs). Every family will face a time when an elder member is unable to care for themselves. Some find solutions by arranging caregiving by family members or hiring help for in-home care. About 5% of people over 65 are now living in some type of long-term care facility. That's about 3.9 million seniors; giving each senior a one-in-four chance of spending time there. But this number dramatically increases for the oldest-old—almost 50% of those 95 and above live in such facilities.[4]

Baby Boomers and their families need to know about the options for senior care. Those wise enough to plan ahead can approach the momentous decision of finding the best place for an aging parent or relative in a proactive way. Following is an in-depth review of the senior care industry that provides information for wise, timely decision-making.

Senior Care Industry Overview

When people think of senior care, what usually comes to mind is a large apartment-type complex that has traditionally been called a "nursing home." For many years, such institutional settings have been the main option for long-term residential care of elders. Because care needs change and vary widely among senior populations, these "nursing homes" offer a range of services that have changed over time with the evolution of the health care industry. A constant and persisting issue is the moving of elders from facility to facility as their needs change, and the institution cannot manage increased levels of care. Seniors who have an accident such as falling and breaking a bone, or who become ill through infection or disease, must be moved to an acute care hospital for awhile. After this hospitalization, the senior goes to a separate rehabilitation facility or sub-unit of a hospital that provides skilled nursing and medical care during recovery. When sufficiently recovered, the senior either moves back into the institution if it can manage current care needs, or goes into another facility that offers a wider range of services.

When seniors have issues with memory or are diagnosed with dementia or Alzheimer's disease, they usually must go into a specialized memory care facility. This could be another wing of a large residential care institution, or a completely separate facility. Every time an elder is moved from setting to setting, this creates emotional trauma and requires adaptations that many elderly simply cannot make very well. The result is a loss in the level of functioning of the senior, as declines in health status later in life do not return to their pre-event levels. With these transitions, lives are cut short, suffering is increased, and costs are continually mounting. Another constant risk is spread of infectious disease among large institutional senior residences. This danger was recently brought into sharp focus by the inequitable spread of COVID-19 infections in senior care facilities, resulting in high mortality rates among elders. In several states, nursing homes accounted for more than half of all COVID-19-related deaths.[5]

> Failure of the health care system to function during crisis was readily apparent in the excess deaths and suffering of seniors in facilities during hurricanes Harvey and Irma in Texas and Florida.
> —Dr. Morris

There are several reasons why this phenomenon occurred in these large institutional facilities. First, there are inconsistencies with which caregiver or other staff is on shift and where. This leads to vulnerable adults being exposed to multiple people. Second, the corporate strategy of having part-time employees causes caregivers to work in multiple facilities or with multiple agencies so that they can get enough hours to meet their financial needs. Finally, the lack of continuity of care and continued training leads to caregivers who master only one or two skills. This can create risks due to inadequate knowledge of preventing spread of infections and use of personal protective equipment. Instead, staff weaknesses should be identified and an effort made to correct these, turning this knowledge into strengths. In general, in large corporate facilities, there is a lack of loyalty and vision for the growth of staff that are essential to the industry. Employers have the notion that there will always be someone else desperate for a job, so there is no need to invest and protect current staff.

Two current trends are reshaping the character of senior care. One is a growing movement toward a more home-like setting and a wider range of options for senior living. The other is the rising acuity levels of residents upon initial move-in across all care segments. Many seniors moving into a facility already have some needs for help with activities of daily living (ADLs). This trend has spurred both independent living and assisted living facilities to provide additional care options to better meet the needs of residents. The facility may incorporate such things as physical therapy and medication administration within its services. Other facilities allow residents to engage third-party service providers to meet care needs that they cannot otherwise offer. This broadens the potential for residents to remain in place while still getting greater care needs met.

Feeding into this acuity level trend is the practice of acute care hospitals to discharge patients at earlier stages of their recovery, putting pressure on skilled nursing facilities and rehabilitation services to take on higher care levels. They are now serving more residents with short-term rehabilitation service needs and those with high-acuity medical care needs, who before spent a longer time recovering in acute care hospitals or in-patient rehabilitation facilities. This trend both increases the cost of skilled nursing facilities and makes them less likely to allow elders with lower care needs or who are not expected to make progress to remain there.

There have been many consequences of these changes in skilled nursing, rehabilitation, and other senior care options. Most of the adverse effects are experienced by an individual and family who are not able to understand the system as a whole, so they cannot anticipate when it will fail them. Because these experiences are so individualized, tracking adverse effects is difficult. However, when the health care system is put under stress during times of crisis, the failure of the system to respond robustly shows overall weakness. In senior care facilities, these failures result from poor planning, poor access to resources, and a system run for profit, not performance.

The Quick Definitions

You'll hear a lot of definitions in the Senior Care Industry and need to learn the acronyms, since everyone uses this alphabet soup as a shortcut. These are quick, short definitions of the wide range of facility types that serve housing and care needs of elders. In the next sections, we will expand on those facilities most closely connected with long-term senior care.

Independent Senior Living (55+ Communities): Retirement developments for seniors have become popular in the past years. These can range from privately owned single residences to condominiums or apartments that are rented. Seniors generally must be able to function independently, though many communities allow residents to employ third-party care providers for in-home assistance. Some of the better known national 55+ communities are Del Webb Sun City, The Villages, Stone Creek, and Holiday Retirement.

Continuing Care Retirement Communities (CCRC): This "all-inclusive" approach has grown recently as seniors seek options to "age in place" without need to move from one senior living community to another. Also called a life plan or tiered community, CCRCs provide the continuum of aging care from independent living, assisted living, skilled nursing care, and memory care within their campus. Seniors must buy into the community, with entry fees ranging from the low to high six figures. There is an additional monthly charge that varies widely among communities, often related to the level of care required.

This can be $5,000 to $9,000 per month. Very few among the U.S. population can afford living in a CCRC.

Skilled Nursing Facilities (SNF): SNF's provide medical and nursing professional care to patients making a transition from an acute care hospital to another facility or back home. They offer rehabilitation and skilled nursing/medical services when patients are recovering from strokes, surgery, or acute illness. These services generally cannot be managed in assisted living facilities. SNFs are not long-term care options, since the length of stay is restricted to 120 days by most insurance.

In-Home Care: Many families choose to provide care for elders themselves, or hire caregivers from the area for varying hours per day. This is still the most widely used option for senior care, at least for several years during the elder's last third of life. As seniors become oldest-old, care needs increase and often cannot be managed in the home setting. Some types of insurance, including Medicaid, will pay family members or others to be in-home caregivers.

Assisted Living Facilities (ALF): ALFs are licensed by the state to provide housing and care to seven or more people in a facility located in a residential neighborhood. These are apartment-style facilities and might have as many as 200 residents, although the average number is around 45. The larger ones often have amenities such as dining rooms, clubhouses, pools, gyms, and meeting rooms. Housing and meals, as well as some assistance with activities of daily living (ADLs), are provided. ALFs may be independently owned or part of a business or corporation.

Adult Family Homes (AFH): An AFH is licensed by the state to provide housing and care for a limited number of unrelated adults in a regular house in a residential neighborhood. The number varies by state with a range between 1 and 8 residents. Some states call these Adult Residential Homes, Group Homes, or Board and Care Homes. These are private homes that have been converted to meet requirements for senior care set by the state. Residents have individual or shared rooms and receive help with ADLs from a trained caregiver. There is staff on-site around the clock. The AFH may be run by a family, individual, or business. Employees of the AFH may be trained to give additional assistance such as following care plans for physical therapy and medication administration, or third-party care can be hired to come in. Some states do not distinguish between ALFs and AFHs in data keeping.

Long-Term Senior Care in ALFs and AFHs

The two types of facilities that provide the bulk of long-term senior care given in other settings than In-Home Care include Assisted Living Facilities (ALFs) and Adult Family Homes (AFHs). Among these two categories are a wide range of options, and there are several key differences:

- ALFs and AFHs are regulated differently by the state.
- ALFs are larger and tend to serve residents who can live more independently.
- ALFs have a greater number of residents and organized activities, offering a wider range of social opportunities.
- ALFs have more caregiver turnover, in the range of 30-40%, reducing the continuity of care.[6]
- ALFs generally move residents to different facilities when higher levels of care are needed.
- ALFs are usually not located in the seniors' home community.

- ALFs accept a wide range of payment options, including Medicaid and many types of insurance.

- ALFs offer investment opportunities only through corporate stock ownership.

- AFHs have higher staff-to-resident ratios offering closer supervision of residents.

- AFHs have lower staff turnover, which increases the continuity of care.

- AFHs have fewer residents and organized activities, reducing social opportunities.

- AFHs serve residents needing higher levels of care, keeping residents in the same home.

- AFHs have less risk of exposure to infections due to small numbers of residents and staff.

- AFHs accept more Medicaid, Veteran's Benefits, and long-term insurance.

- AFHs are generally located in the senior's home community.

- AFHs offer direct personal investment opportunities for individuals and families to become Owner-Operators. This includes franchise opportunities (see Chapter 3).

In the next sections, we will examine these and other differences in greater detail. Whether you are looking into senior care options for yourself or your parents, it's important to learn as much as possible about advantages and disadvantages of these two types of long-term care. Keep this information within the context of good stewardship, your responsibility to handle family properties and resources in a way that derives the most benefits.

One significant point to remember within the stewardship context is that there is no future for augmenting family finances through Assisted Living Facilities. Most likely, you or your family will not own one of these larger facilities; this is the realm of corporate ownership. By becoming involved in Adult Family Homes for senior care, however, you have the potential to become an owner of one or more homes, or part of a franchise that might own many homes. As we will see in later chapters, owning and/or operating an Adult Family Home is a profitable business that increases property value and brings a steady income stream.

Another critical consideration involves rates of infection in these two types of facilities. Even before the outbreak of the COVID-19 pandemic in early 2020, ALFs were known for increased risk of infections of various types. Whenever high-risk elders are congregated in confined spaces and exposed to significant numbers of caregivers who also work in other facilities, there is danger of infection transmission. The COVID-19 pandemic spread widely among ALFs, causing high death rates among elders. Although fewer than 1% of Americans live in long-term care facilities, over 40% of COVID-19 deaths have occurred there. By mid-November 2020, over 94,000 deaths had occurred among residents and workers in these facilities. The tragic toll of this pandemic in these settings can be attributed primarily to an outdated and flawed infrastructure and inability to foresee a health storm of this magnitude. Inadequate responses from business owners and government officials also played major parts. Highlighting these inadequacies, a report by the GAO (U.S. Government Accountability Office) in May 2020, found that 82% of nursing homes had been cited for infection-control deficiencies before the pandemic.[7]

Because AFHs are small, with between 1 and 8 residents by state law, and staff numbers and turnover are less, the risk of infection exposure is greatly reduced. For families of vulnerable seniors, there is immense relief in knowing that the risk of contracting an infection is lower when they place a beloved parent in an Adult Family Home.

Assisted Living Facilities

ALFs are also known as congregate housing, residential care, adult congregate care, boarding home, assisted living residence, or domiciliary care. These facilities provide a group living environment and typically cater to an older adult population. They also serve adults over 18 with disabilities. Their purpose is to provide care and housing for adults who cannot or choose not to live independently. They are generally suitable for people who need little daily care, although there is much variation in the types of nursing care and assistance with ADLs that individual ALFs offer.

ALFs have roots prior to 1965 in boarding homes and philanthropically funded facilities called "homes for the aged." After the advent of Medicare and Medicaid in that year, many homes for the aged converted to licensed nursing facilities encouraged by federal funding. These nursing homes became more hospital-like over time, offering higher health care levels, and gradually evolved into Skilled Nursing Facilities. Some residential care facilities did not convert, either not meeting regulatory standards, or choosing to remain unlicensed. These were called rest homes, retirement homes, adult care homes, and convalescent homes, among others. Some settings targeted low-income elders who needed some help with room and board, using a minimalist approach to board-and-care that was colloquially called *"three hots and a cot."*

During the 1980s and 1990s, several models of assisted living emerged. These varied according to how much emphasis was given to: hospitality—the retirement community model, mostly focused on independent living with group amenities; housing—the group living model which focused on keeping elders functional and delaying placement in higher care level facilities; health care model—offering more nursing services and often integrating independent housing with existing nursing facilities; hybrid—a blended model emphasizing residential-style settings, variable service capacity, and a philosophy of consumer autonomy.

The complex assisted living industry received an infusion of various funding sources, faced problems with lack of uniform standards, and weathered controversy due to reports of neglect, abuse, and mistreatment of residents. In the U.S., ALFs can be owned by for-profit companies (publicly traded or LLCs), nonprofit organizations, or governments. Many Operators faced the realities of cash flow due to expensive systems development, training, and management issues. Some found it difficult to sustain espoused values for assisted living, as issues of safety collided with goals of autonomy. There followed a crisis of confidence fueled by investigations of mistreatment and mismanagement in the early 2000s.[8]

At present, nearly 1.2 million people live in around 30,000 ALFs in the U.S. The typical resident is an 80-year-old mobile female with an average annual income of about $30,000. She would have recently moved from a private home and will remain in the ALF on average for two to three years. After this time, many residents move from the ALF because they need acute hospital care, run into financial problems, need higher levels of care at a Skilled Nursing Facility or memory care unit, or return home.[9]

> An elderly person with significant health problems receives optimum care when there is consistency of care. This means being cared for by the same providers, in the same care facility, with the continuous support of family.
> —Dr. Morris

Residents in ALFs usually have their own private or semi-private apartments, which include bedroom, kitchen area, and bathroom. Many are able to lock their doors for privacy. Some may be in dormitory-style bedrooms or use shared bathrooms. Most are allowed to have small pets, use tobacco and consume alcohol, and have visitors any time during the day, as well as overnight guests. In larger facilities, there are group amenities such as dining options, gyms, pools, activities, clubs, meeting rooms, and even beauty salons. Usually, these facilities offer housekeeping and maintenance, laundry services, transportation, emergency call systems in both private and common areas, 24-hour security, social services, and religious activities. Depending upon state requirements, they provide assistance with daily living activities (bathing, eating, dressing, toileting, etc.) and health services with medication administration. The majority of ALFs contract with home health agencies to provide skilled nursing care, and with hospice providers for end of life care.

In these large facilities, there is a wide range of socialization opportunities. Most have regular activities, clubs, programs, field trips, and other ways that seniors can gather in groups with similar interests. With a large number of residents, seniors can more readily find others with shared hobbies, values, and preferences. Options for friendships are usually plentiful. Having good social networks and frequent interactions is associated with increased wellbeing and appears to enhance overall health.

The goal of ALFs is to help people remain independent as long as possible in an environment that supports their choice, dignity, autonomy, privacy, and safety. They emphasize family and community involvement, with the intention that when residents have temporary incapacity, they remain in the facility if possible, or return after necessary outside services have been provided. This is not always possible; however, depending on the extent of services each

ALF is capable of providing. As aging progresses, care needs should be reevaluated on a regular basis, and modifications made in the service program as needed. When care needs increase, additional costs are involved, which can strain family finances if not planned for in advance.

Costs of ALFs vary according to the range of services offered and payment methods accepted. In general, fees charged for an ALF pay for housing in the facility and some services. Families should meet with an ALF coordinator and have an initial evaluation to determine what services the elder will need. Specific services differ greatly, so fees will also be different among facilities. Some ALFs offer an all-inclusive monthly price, with tiered pricing based on required services or for individual services requested by the resident. On average, fees range from $2,000 to $4,000 per month or more, depending on services offered, location, size, and availability.

Most residents of ALFs pay privately, either with their own or family resources. Some states provide public assistance through Medicaid, Supplementary Security Income (SSI), or Social Services Block Grant programs. Most states subsidizing these assisted living services do so using Medicaid 1915c waivers. These waivers are only available to people meeting state criteria for "nursing home care," which is a higher level of care needs. There is limited access to such public assistance programs. Some states also have other strategies to help lower costs of assisted living, including Low-Income Housing Tax Credits, bonds, and others. While private long-term care insurance and some managed care programs may also assist with ALF expenses, Medicare does not cover them.

Medicare was never designed to cover the costs of long-term care, but to meet the medical needs of seniors. Long-term care includes non-medical care for people who have a chronic illness or disability; it includes non-skilled personal care assistance, such as help with ADLs. Specifically excluded from Medicare coverage are: dressing, bathing, using the bathroom, home-delivered meals, and adult day health care. These things are considered "custodial care" and thus are not medical services. Long-term care services may be paid through Medicaid (if the senior qualifies) or seniors can buy private long-term care insurance.[10]

It is sometimes confusing because of the coverage Medicare provides for skilled nursing facility care. Regardless of where the senior is residing when illness or injury occurs, Medicare covers medically necessary services and supplies in a skilled nursing facility. The patient first must have a 3-day minimum, medically necessary, inpatient hospital stay for a related illness or injury. Those with Medicare Advantage Plan may not need a 3-day hospital stay. To remain in a skilled nursing facility, the care provided must be necessary to improve or maintain your current condition. If the facility decides you are not making improvements, or no longer require skilled nursing care, you will be discharged. Coverage is structured to pay in full for the first 20 days, partly with coinsurance for days 21-100, and nothing after day 100 of each benefit period.

While ALF monthly costs for minimal care may be affordable for most, as care needs of elders increase, monthly costs will also rise. Especially costly is the situation when an elder crosses the "dementia divide" and requires constant supervision and safety measures. Even if they remain in the same facility, costs now rise to $8,000 - $10,000 per month. These spiraling costs are the primary reason most people will spend much of their estate in the final three years of their lives. Letting an estate be eroded away in this manner is not good stewardship.

The assisted living industry is a segment of the senior housing industry, and ALFs can be stand-alone facilities or part of multi-level senior living communities. It exemplifies the shift from "care as service" to "care as business." The industry is dominated by for-profit businesses; nearly 70% of seniors housing and care properties are for-profit entities. Only a small number of the top seventy largest operators are nonprofit. Across the ALF community specifically, 10% of total units are owned by nonprofits while the remaining 90% are owned by for-profit entities.[11] It is a consumer-driven industry with a wide range of options, levels of care, and diversity of services. It is regulated at the state, not national, level and definitions of ALFs vary by both state and organization running the business.

Adult Family Homes

Adult Family Homes offer an attractive option for long-term senior care. These are residential homes licensed by a state authority to provide personal care for up to eight non-related individuals (called "residents"). These homes are located in residential neighborhoods and provide personal care and supervision, medication assistance, and help with ADLs such as grooming, bathing, dressing, and incontinence care. Room and board are included, and other services such as laundry are common. Many AFHs also have social activities and transportation to shopping and doctors.

The concept of a group of elders living together in a residential-type home has existed for many years. These were called adult care homes, personal care homes, adult foster homes, and residential care homes. During the 1970s and 1980s, they differentiated from nursing homes, which were increasingly institutional due to government regulations following the enactment of Medicare and Medicaid. AFHs are distinct from ALFs because of their small size and home-like setting, although both are part of the senior long-term care industry. Limiting the number of residents helps maintain the family atmosphere of AFHs, and their locations enhance a sense of neighborhood living.

Washington State first introduced regulations for AFHs around 1986 and began licensing them in 1989. Other states such as Oregon were also early adopters of this model for elder care, where the resident limit is five adults. Currently, state regulation, oversight, and supervision have expanded, and the process of becoming a licensed AFH is complex. Both the home and the Owner must be licensed. Private residences that are converted into AFHs, as well as new constructions, must meet structural and safety requirements. Each AFH has a business Owner and an Operator. Sometimes this is the same person. The AFH may be operated by a single person, married couple, or family who also live in the home with residents. Or, the Operator might be a business that hires employees to be managers or caregivers. There must be a staff member in the home 24/7, but they do not need to reside in the facility. Some AFHs have caregivers in the facility around the clock who stay in a room provided, but do not live there. The Owner/Operator must be available by phone in case of emergencies.

The Owner/Operator is responsible for compliance with all state rules and regulations. Some homes are operated by registered nurses or other medical professionals, but this is not required. All Owners/Operators and staff receive training prior to having contact with residents, and must complete additional training each year.

> Most U.S. adults choose not to live in communal living situations: homes where several families share living spaces and kitchens are not common. One benefit of AFHs is their similarity to the typical American home with small numbers in a single dwelling. Most large corporate ALFs have a sterile institutional feel, just the opposite of the warm home environment the seniors have been in the entirety of their lives.
> —Dr. Morris

Once homes are in business, they have unannounced inspections by the state that include a review of residential records, medication logs, physician orders, written care plans, change of condition notes, contracts, and safety measures.

AFHs have been considered among the least expensive and most flexible options for long-term care of the aging population. They have great appeal for most seniors and their families because of the home-like setting that is familar and secure. Some of the key benefits include:

- Family-oriented environment that is small and intimate, especially when Owners live in the home.

- Shared home-cooked meals served in a family-like setting.

- Residential neighborhood that can be in the same area the elder lived in before, or similar.

- Personalized care and better ability to cater to individual needs.

- Closer supervision and familiarity of staff with each resident.

- Greater ability of staff to recognize small changes in status due to familiarity with the residents.

- Quick action when changes are noticed and additional care is needed.

- Higher levels of care can be arranged as elders' needs increase within the same setting.

- Better staff-to-resident ratios (1 staff to 6 residents at minimum in AFH, compared to 1 staff to as many as 10-15 residents in ALFs)

- Enhanced safety during epidemics due to the ability to quickly lock down and decrease exposure from staff (fewer staff members, less turnover, less dual employment).

AFHs can also specialize in the types of residents they wish to attract and the extent of care services they provide. Some homes focus on veterans or ethnic groups, offering opportunities to socialize with others who share many values and experiences. Other homes focus on special care needs, such as residents with dementia, mental illness, or developmental disabilities. If a nurse is an Owner, Operator or staff member, the home can offer higher-level care that meets more extensive medical needs.

Costs of AFHs range between $3,000 to $8,000 per month, depending on the extent of services provided and type of facility rooms. Most payment methods associated with long-term care are accepted. Currently, Medicare does not cover care in Adult Family Homes. Many AFHs do accept Medicaid when seniors meet specified income eligibility requirements. Facilities accepting Medicaid usually limit the number of beds/rooms allotted to this form of payment, and the services and rooms are on the lower side. This can be very bleak and the range of services quite small. Veteran's benefits pay for a portion of long-term care, but not enough to cover 100%. Private pay is a common method used, but can eat up savings and assets quickly. Some seniors resort to reverse mortgages that are based on age and the value of their home. These last two approaches continually reduce the value of home assets and are not satisfactory approaches to good stewardship.

Seniors with long-term care insurance can use this payment form, depending on specific requirements and guidelines of their policies. Some may have life insurance policies that cover specified long-term care services and locations, or an accelerated death benefit used in the event of a terminal illness diagnosis. A life settlement, which is selling a life insurance policy to a third party, can be used

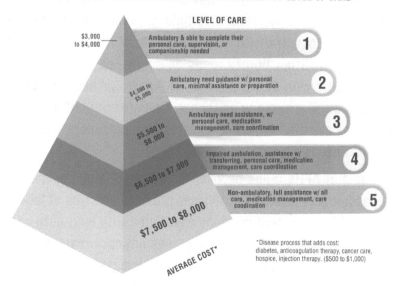

COSTS OF ADULT FAMILY HOMES ACCORDING TO LEVEL OF CARE

LEVEL OF CARE

$3,000 to $4,000 — Ambulatory & able to complete their personal care, supervision, or companionship needed **1**

Ambulatory need guidance w/ personal care, minimal assistance or preparation **2** — $4,500 to $5,000

Ambulatory need assistance, w/ personal care, medication management, care coordination **3** — $5,500 to $6,000

Impaired ambulation, assistance w/ transferring, personal care, medication management, care coordination **4** — $6,500 to $7,000

Non-ambulatory, full assistance w/ all care, medication management, care coodination **5**

$7,500 to $8,000

AVERAGE COST*

*Disease process that adds cost: diabetes, anticoagulation therapy, cancer care, hospice, injection therapy. ($500 to $1,000)

for paying long-term care costs. The third-party purchaser pays a value exceeding the policy's cash surrender value, but less than its face value or death benefit.

Not all AFHs will accept every form of payment. Especially if using Medicaid, Veteran's Benefits, and long-term insurance, be sure the home you choose takes that method of payment. It's important to check into the stipulations attached to these options in advance of making a decision. Some have age requirements or restrictions; some require that you be healthy, while others can only be used after an illness has developed or become terminal.[12]

Referral Agents

The senior care industry has become vast and complex, so it's helpful to seek advice and information when looking for a placement for your parents or yourself. Most state health and human services departments have senior care divisions that will offer resources and, at times, a counselor or advocate who will assist in finding the right senior facility. In addition, there are many organizations that have formed to support consumers looking for placements. Some organizations are nonprofit and consumer-run, while others are for-profit businesses.

Referral agents work by contracts with certain AFHs and are paid by commission. Thus, the list of homes they might recommend is limited by those with whom they have contracts. This might lead to placement of seniors in a home that does not fully meet their needs. The Operator of the AFH generally pays the agent 100% of the resident's first month's rent; this could be a $3,000-8,000 fee. Payment may be the total upfront or prorated over three months. At times the senior may be moved if the current home does not work out, or the agent has located a better one. When elderly people are uprooted too often, they suffer confusion and stress, often with harmful effects on health and mental status.

Services of referral agents are certainly not "free" since the AFH Operator must pay fees. Not all referral agencies operate for profit, however, even though they may have fees for services. Below are examples of state and national agencies that can assist families and elders to find a suitable AFH.

> Services of referral agents are not "free" since the AFH operator must pay fees, usually the amount of the first month's rent. Agents work by contracts with certain AFHs and get commissions when they refer a client. This narrows the choices for clients and families.

The **Association of Senior Referral Professionals** (ASRP) is an organization of individuals and businesses who offer referral services to the senior housing and care industry in Washington

State. It is committed to establishing and promoting professional and ethical standards within the senior housing and care referral industry, as well as to those who provide supportive and ancillary services for older and other frail adults. This group publishes materials that give a unified approach to ethical standards, recommended best practices, education for increasing knowledge and skills, education to increase consumer awareness, feedback and referral channels, consumer protection, and collaboration for consumers and members of the association to have a voice in future legislation and regulation regarding senior housing and care services.

The **Adult Family Home Council** (AFHC) of WA is a mission-driven member organization formed in 1995 with the purpose of providing AFH Operators with resources and training in all aspects of their business. It advocates on behalf of AFH Operators with the state legislature, the Department of Social and Health Services, as a member of the WA State Senior Citizen's Lobby, and is the representative of AFHs for collective bargaining. The Council sets standards of practice for AFH Operators and training requirements, offers continuing education, information, and networking opportunities. It has published guidelines for selecting an AFH, cost data, and additional resources.

There are a number of private referral agencies that will work with seniors and their families seeking a placement for long-term living. A simple internet search will connect you to several options. The main goal is to help residents maintain independence while receiving quality care and protecting the resident's rights. "A Place for Mom" is a senior care referral agency with nationwide services that are free to the family. Their goal is to help seniors and families find the best fit with an AFH in their area. Most states have branches of these groups or similar organizations.

With over 3,200 AFHs to choose from in Washington state providing care to more than 19,000 seniors,[13] working with a referral agent can be an excellent choice to find the one that best meets each senior and family's criteria. It's always a good idea to talk to friends or acquaintances who have gone through this process and learn from their experiences. When considering a particular set of AFHs, you can make a list of the pros and cons of each option. Studying this list against your own criteria will help you choose the right AFH for your family situation.

Each state has its agencies that provide information and assistance in finding senior assisted living options. National organizations also offer counseling and recommendations, such as the American Association of Retired Persons (AARP), The National Center for Assisted Living (NCAL) of the American Health Care Association (AHCA), the American Seniors Housing Association, American Geriatrics Society, and the U.S. National Institute on Health-Institute on Aging-Senior Health.

The small, intimate, residential, home-like feel of an AFH may be the right option for your parents, loved ones, or yourself. Each AFH is unique, so take time to do adequate research, evaluate care needs today, and try to anticipate changes in those care needs in the future. You will want an AFH that has the capability to deal with future needs, not just those currently present. Conversations with the AFH Operator and staff should include not only these care needs, but the social, cultural, and spiritual environment of their home.

It is important to ask the right questions. Here are some of the questions to consider that have been suggested by organizations and referral agents:

Each senior and family will have their own questions related to personal needs and preferences. Make a thorough list and bring it with you when visiting potential homes. Because AFHs are smaller and often Owner-operated, there is usually a great deal of flexibility in being able to provide individualized services. Of course, have a thorough discussion about fees and provisions for increasing care needs. Ask what is included in the base fee and what additional charges might be per month when care needs change.

Two Scenarios: The Bad and the Good When Seniors Need Medical Care

From the emergency medicine viewpoint, senior care is extremely variable. First responders and emergency room staff understand which senior facilities provide good care by how they present the patient when acute care in the hospital is needed. Typical good and bad examples follow.
—Dr. Morris

When making decisions about which senior living facility to select, it's important to keep in mind how the facility will perform when their residents need medical attention. There will be times when the elder becomes ill, assessments must be made, and decisions taken about when, where, and how to get the necessary medical care. The quality and nature of staffing, familiarity with residents, and organization protocols all play important roles when emergency care is needed.

How long has the AFH
been in operation?

How many staff are
typically on shift?

Will there be staff awake
at night?

Are pets allowed?

Is the location close
enough for regular
family visits?

Will the type of food served,
and the dining setting, meet
needs and preferences?

Do some staff speak
your primary language?

What activities are regularly
arranged for residents?

What is the
staff-to-resident
ratio?

Are the grounds
pleasant and
accessible?

Will you or your loved one
have a good fit with other
residents?

What is the highest level of
care that this AFH can
accommodate?

Are transportation services
available?

Bad Scenario

An 80-year-old woman arrives at the emergency room by ambulance at midnight. Her chief complaint (presenting problem) is altered mental status (confusion).

She arrives alone. The ambulance staff summoned to her facility were met by a clerk who did not know anything about her or why the ambulance was called. Facility caregivers had gone home shortly after calling the ambulance. The patient has dementia and cannot give a history.

The ambulance transports her to a convenient hospital, having no information about where she usually gets medical care. It happens to be in a different health care system than the one where she received care most of her life. The two systems do not share information.

The clinical staff in the emergency room have NO information. Paperwork from the facility does not contain any useful information (medication list, health history, family or medical contacts). They have nothing about patient wishes such as End of Life Directives and No Not Resuscitate orders.

Good Scenario

An 80-year-old woman arrives at the emergency room by ambulance at midnight. Her chief complaint (presenting problem) is altered mental status (confusion).

A caregiver from the facility arrives with the patient and provides a history, helps with the patient's care, and reassures the patient in the unsettling emergency room environment. The caregiver has known the woman for years, is the residential director of the facility, and lives in the same house.

The caregiver directed the ambulance to the health care system hospital where the patient received care her whole life. Written records are given to emergency room staff with the patient's health history, medication list, and medical care preferences.

The clinical staff in the emergency room has access to the patients' clinic and hospital notes, being in the same system. They ask questions of the caregiver to gather recent information about the patient's current problem, and verify any recent changes to care regimens.

They call the facility but there is no answer; the clerk has gone home for the night. Not knowing the patient's normal mental status and with no options, the ER doctor orders an exhaustive, expensive, and uncomfortable medical workup (blood work, ECG, Chest X-ray, CT scans, urinary catheter).

A urinary tract infection is identified; the patient is given broad spectrum instead of tailored antibiotics because prior antibiotic sensitivities are not known, increasing risk of side effects.

Since the patient's facility could not be contacted, she was unnecessarily admitted to the hospital. When contact was made the next morning, the doctor learned that the patient has frequent urinary tract infections that worsen her confusion. In addition, she is near the end of her life and had requested no invasive interventions such as blood draws.

The caregiver had called the patient's family when it became necessary for the emergency room visit. The family remains in cellphone contact with the caregiver, whom they have known for years, trust, and have a warm personal relationship with. Together a decision is made that the family need not make the two-hour drive to the emergency department.

With a good history, notes, and examination, the doctor decides this is probably a urinary tract infection. A urinalysis confirms it and a tailored antibiotic is given, based on review of prior sensitivities and efficacy.

The doctor wanted to do blood tests, but the caregiver said due to the patient's dislike of needles she has requested no blood draws unless it is a life-threatening emergency. The patient is discharged from the emergency room two hours later since it is clear that no hospitalization is needed. Another caregiver picks up the patient in a private vehicle and takes her back to the facility.

These two scenarios are not atypical for senior visits to the emergency department. It is clear which is preferable and results in better outcomes for the senior and health care system. Familiarity with the senior, knowledge of health conditions, and close supervision are essential for high-quality care. While both scenarios are possible in any type of facility, the nature of the senior care facility design makes the good scenario more likely in an Adult Family Home.

The Next Step:
Investing in Adult Family Homes

Now that you have a basis for understanding the senior care industry and the options available to your family, with an emphasis on the advantages of Adult Family Homes, it's time to turn to a different perspective on financial aspects. You have learned that AFHs as an investment opportunity can offer a continuing income stream as well as make provisions for your parents' (and your own) future senior living needs. Wouldn't it be great to avoid having worries about where and how living and care needs would be met during the last third of life, and at the same time having dollars flowing in vs. out for senior care?

Investing in AFHs can be a solution to these worries. There are great opportunities for investors with different goals and motives in the realm of Adult Family Homes. The specifics of these opportunities are explored in the following chapter.

3

AFH INVESTOR SCENARIOS

IF YOU ASKED people with interest in real estate investing where would be a good place to put your money, few would first think about the senior housing and care market. But, they would be missing a great opportunity for profitable investing! Savvy investors have found that the combined components of real estate, hospitality, and needs-driven services give senior housing and care properties a unique advantage. This combination offers the benefits of real estate investment along with the characteristics of the health care field, providing unusual resiliency through economic cycles. This resiliency was clear during the real estate downturn of 2008-2009 when senior housing and care properties outperformed other commercial real estate property in terms of return on investment (ROI) and rent growth.

The senior housing and care sector of real estate investing includes an array of housing and service types. It is generally divided into four categories:

- Independent living
- Assisted living

- Memory care
- Nursing care

What the National Investment Center for Seniors Housing & Health Care (NIC) calls the "investment-grade seniors housing and care property market" includes institutions that offer the above types of care to seniors, either as one segment or a combination. The trend is toward a more homelike setting, even for nursing care, and many institutions provide care in a multifamily setting. Life Plan Communities (Continuing Care Retirement Communities—CCRCs) that offer at least two care segments are included. However, as used by the NIC, 55+ independent living communities that do not provide other care segments are not included.

Adult Family Homes are also excluded from this market by NIC definitions, but should be considered an attractive real estate investment. Owning one or more AFHs can provide a continuing income stream and grow the worth of your investment. Most of the characteristics that make the senior housing and care property market a good investment also apply to AFHs. This is a steadily growing real estate segment driven by population statistics and continuing needs of elders for health care and living assistance as they age.

As an example of the scope of the senior housing and care sector, in 2017, the NIC reported there were 23,500 "investment-grade" properties containing 3 million units with an estimated total market capitalization of $409 billion. This is a robust market that reported over 3,700 distinct transactions through the year end of 2017 of properties valued at $2.5 million minimum, representing over $138 billion in closed transactions volume.

The factors affecting demand for senior housing and care properties include demographics, labor market conditions, economic cycles, occupancy rates, and the housing market. The major drivers of demand are influenced by seniors' age and need for assistance, their net worth and income, and their knowledge about and desire for some form of senior housing and care. Adult children often have important roles in creating this demand. Their elderly parents or relatives frequently turn to them for help, or they are drawn into the process by observing that the elders cannot continue to live in the current setting. Decisions to seek senior housing and care are often influenced by adult children's opinions and financial resources.

Although we've already looked at demographics of the elderly U.S. population, it's worth revisiting in light of the Baby Boomer effect. The oldest Baby Boomers (born in 1946) have just begun reaching 74 years of age in 2020. The average move-in age for senior housing is the mid-80s. So, the Baby Boomers will not begin reaching this average move-in age for at least 10 years. When that happens, watch for a surge—the Baby Boomers will significantly drive up demand for senior housing and care.

Currently, the parents of Baby Boomers and the generation before are already driving up demand for senior housing and care. The 80+ and 85+ populations are predicted to increase steadily for the rest of this decade. In the next decade, growth of these groups will accelerate. Focusing upon the seniors ages 82 to 86, the time period they are most likely to move into assisted living facilities, an even steeper rise is projected. By the late 2020s and into the next decade, this age group is expected to increase an average of 5.3% per year. Not only are more people reaching their 80s and beyond, once attaining that age, they are living more additional years.

If the 82- to 86-year-old cohort increases 5.3% per year for 10 years, this results in an overall increase of more than 50%.

That includes the base population plus half again as many elders for assisted living facilities to serve. To get a sense of the need and demand for senior housing and care, take into account that a man who is 85 years old is expected to live an additional 5.9 years, and a woman age 85 to live another 7.0 years.[1]

Move-in age group (82-86 years) increases 5.3% per year (>50% increase in 10 years)

- 85-year-old man lives another 5.9 years

- 85-year-old woman lives another 7.0 years

These factors make it clear that demand for senior housing and care is on a steadily rising projection. More capacity will be needed both in the "investment-grade" properties and in the more personalized and flexible Adult Family Homes segment. Now is an excellent time to invest in this growing and profitable sector.

Investment Options in Adult Family Homes

You can become involved as an investor in Adult Family Homes in several ways. The route you choose depends upon your personal interests and goals. The simplest route is to buy into real estate groups or organizations that own or finance one or more AFHs. Your primary goal is to increase the value of your assets and earn a good return on investment. Your involvement will be minimal, like a stockholder in a corporation. You invest money, the organization uses that money to buy and operate the AFHs, and you receive returns by monthly payouts as the value of the real estate increases. These are the real estate investors.

Another route is to invest in organizations that own and operate AFHs, but your motive for selecting them is to use your resources for the greater good of society and the environment. Some environmental benefits of AFHs include reduced carbon footprint and investing, buying, and employing locally. For some people, knowing how much AFHs contribute to the wellbeing of their residents and bolster the economy of local communities are underlying reasons for their choice of investing in this type of real estate.

A third route for investors may be the desire to support building a like-minded community. It really is true that "birds of a feather flock together." Creating an AFH focused on bringing together those who belong to a certain religious group, or ethnic nationality, or even share special interests is proving to be an increasingly attractive option for seniors. It is comforting for elders to live among others with whom they feel familiar; often expressed as being around folks "like me." There are currently adult family homes for Mandarin-speaking Chinese, Koreans, Lutherans, Vietnam War veterans, and others. Things such as shared language, cuisines, and customs are very meaningful to quality of life.

Finally, investing in AFHs can be motivated by the desire to be a good family care steward by creating a legacy, keeping assets in the family. When you follow this route, your main goal is to preserve and enhance the worth of your family's financial situation. You see investing in an AFH as a method for expanding the value of family property, such as converting Mom and Dad's home into an income-generating property. It also will grow family assets and provide an income stream that will cover the costs of their housing and care during the last third of life. This increasingly valuable real estate will also serve as a family inheritance that endures years beyond their passing. These are the family legacy investors.

Some Thoughts Regarding Legacy

Across the globe, concepts of family and home are quite variable. In most cultures, the family is more involved in care of the elderly than in the United States, where personal care of elders is generally done by people outside the family unit. This is likely related to the long work hours expected in the U.S. and fewer multigenerational households. Thus, many U.S. families experience disconnection when their elders enter some form of assisted living. They are less familiar with underlying health concerns of elders, and less able to recognize subtle behavioral changes pointing to greater care needs. They may also be unfamiliar with the elders' desires regarding inheritance, managing assets, and end of life preferences.

It is difficult to create an enduring legacy when families are disconnected from their elders. An important benefit of the planning process for senior care and housing is that it puts families back in close contact with the seniors. Even though having to grapple with decisions about where to place Mom or Dad can be challenging, it can also be unifying.

The issue that many Baby Boomer households now face of deciding where loved ones should reside touches many areas. The area of finances is usually a major factor.

Baby Boomers are often referred to as "The Sandwich Generation." Their households are typically positioned directly in the middle of caring for the housing needs of their parents' generation and those of their

> Baby Boomers are called "The Sandwich Generation" because they have responsibilities both for young adult children and aging parents. Inter-generational changes place stress on Boomers who often have their own health, career, and financial issues.
> —Dr. Morris

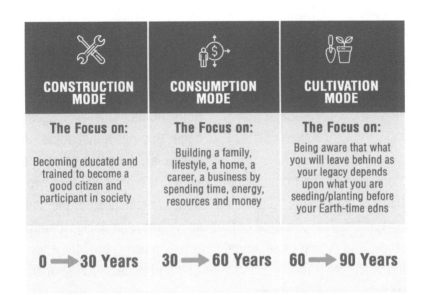

CONSTRUCTION MODE	CONSUMPTION MODE	CULTIVATION MODE
The Focus on:	**The Focus on:**	**The Focus on:**
Becoming educated and trained to become a good citizen and participant in society	Building a family, lifestyle, a home, a career, a business by spending time, energy, resources and money	Being aware that what you will leave behind as your legacy depends upon what you are seeding/planting before your Earth-time edns
0 ➡ 30 Years	30 ➡ 60 Years	60 ➡ 90 Years

adult children's generation. In addition, Boomers must consider their own final third of life planning. All of these represent substantial financial commitment and management.

Take, for example, the scenario in which the estate created by grandparents must be tapped in order to fund their move into assisted living. Those dollars, which Gramma and Grampa preserved with the hope of funding the college education of their grandchildren, are now flowing in a different direction. Three generations are financially impacted by these decisions. Thus, the importance of considering all options for senior housing and care becomes abundantly clear. This reinforces the principle of what it means to be good stewards of the resources entrusted and underlines serious consideration of what kind of legacy is being formed.

There is a scene in the Broadway play "Hamilton" in which the title character talks about legacy as "planting seeds for which one will not see, or taste the fruit of." This beautifully sums up the reality

During this time, Boomer households must progress from the modes of "Construction" and "Consumption" typical of the first two-thirds of life into the "Cultivation" mode of the final third of life.

that the decisions and actions you take today will send out waves that impact, shape, and change the balance for future households. This awareness helps Boomer households, in particular, progress from the "Construction and Consumption" mode that typifies the first two-thirds of life into the "Cultivation" mode characteristic of the final third of life. This is a time of thinking, willing, and doing. It spurs people into paying close attention to how much "seed" they have and where they should plant it for getting the best "fruit," or the greatest increase of assets.

Levels of Involvement for AFH Investors

People who invest in AFHs can choose their level of involvement in the operations of the facilities. A pure Investor would be someone who only contributes money to a home, group, or organization but does not become involved in AFH operations. Those who want closer involvement in managing the AFH are generally considered to be Operators or Owners of AFH services. In this role, you are both investing money and overseeing the operations of an AFH or group of homes. This could also be a business that hires employees to be managers and caregivers. The level of greatest involvement comes when you are an Investor, Operator, and Owner of an AFH. Then, you often live on-site and supervise the day-to-day operations, interacting closely with residents and caregiving staff. Some Owner/Operators take on the role of caregivers themselves as a way to be involved. This helps them make sure the standard of care is consistent with their expectations.

Here is a quick summary of AFH roles and levels of involvement:

- **Investor:** Puts money into AFHs.

- **Owner:** Owns an AFH business (may or may not be Operator).

- **Operator:** Runs an AFH business (may or may not be Owner)

- **Owner/Operator:** AFH owner who also operates the business.

- **Resident Manager:** day-to-day manager of AFH; best practice is to live in the home, but this is not required.

- **Caregiver:** provides direct care to AFH residents.

Whichever investment option you select, you can be assured that AFHs are excellent vehicles for growing assets and creating financial security. Your motivation for investing in AFHs will help determine the type of relationship you have with the business. There are three basic investor motivations that focus on growing real estate assets, having a positive social impact, and creating a family legacy through good stewardship of resources. The following section examines these three basic types of AFH investor profiles in greater depth.

AFH Investor Profiles

Motivations for investing in the AFH business cluster people into the following three profiles.

AFH INVESTOR PROFILES

The Real Estate Investor

This group of investors ranges from individuals to large multi-national corporations. As those investing in rental real estate know, the bottom line is finding and keeping good tenants. These tenants must have good leases that allow Owners to maintain and improve the value of the real estate asset. Tenants must pay rent on time, take care of the property as they use it, and notify Owners promptly of structural and functional problems. To make rental real estate profitable, tenants must operate successful businesses or be capable of paying increased rent to absorb rising costs if they occupy homes or apartments. Savvy real estate investors know that crunching the numbers is essential. They must consider things like vacancy rates, net profits, internal rate of return, tax strategies, depreciation, appreciation, and a host of other factors depending upon the nature of the rentals.

Adult Family Homes, as a sector of the seniors housing and care market, offer what some call "The Holy Grail" of real estate investing. The foundation for this is the stable and reliable nature of elders as renters. Value is enhanced by the growing need for senior housing and care based on U.S. population demographics. These factors combine to produce a stable, responsible tenant who will pay more than the going market rate, will sign a long-term and favorable lease, and will take responsibility for the maintenance and repair of the real estate. In most instances, the real estate is located in neighborhood areas with higher-than-average appreciation.

It might sound too good to be true, but with AFHs, this is precisely the scenario! These characteristics make AFHs very appealing to those who want to grow their money through real estate.

The Social Impact Investor

The primary motivation for this group of investors is to put their money to work for positive social and environmental impact. When making decisions about how we earn, spend, and invest our money, many of us take into consideration the positive or negative effect it will have on others and the planet. If these are some of your concerns, you make career choices based on whether or not your conscience will allow you to participate in that particular field or business endeavor. You usually make purchase decisions based on whether it's good for society, the natural world, and the planet overall. Many of us do this, whether it's something as big as buying a new car or as small as a bag of chips.

The social impact investor wants dollars invested to support businesses, companies, and groups that have a positive social impact or are cause-related. A good example of this kind of business, and one that many folks resonate with, is Whole Foods stores. The CEO of Whole Foods, John Mackey, wrote in his best-selling book *Conscious Capitalism*: "It's humbling now to think about what would have happened if all our stakeholders hadn't cared so much about the company, and that we were actually making an important difference in people's lives. A company that . . . would have died in its first year if our stakeholders hadn't loved and cared about it."[2]

The plight of many elders in our society has spurred widespread concern, especially among socially conscious people. We hear tragic stories about seniors with nowhere to go once they cannot maintain themselves at home. There are grim facts about elder poverty and abusive treatment. According to the National Council on Aging, 1 in 10 Americans over age 60 experience some form of elder abuse, including financial exploitation, willful deprivation, passive neglect, and confinement. Two-thirds of the perpetrators are adult children or spouses, for many people honestly don't know what to do with their aging parents. Sadly, it is estimated that only 1 in 14 cases of elder abuse are reported to authorities.[3]

There must be a better way to take care of seniors, one that doesn't involve keeping them at home with an ill-equipped family or sinking their entire life savings into corporate-run assisted living. Many seniors and their families have only known about one option: first, a retirement community, and then an assisted living facility. This type of thinking was ingrained into our minds by corporate America, since most major companies set retirees up with a 401K to cash out when reaching age 55+ and live on for the rest of their lives. But, in order for that system to work, you must have upward of $500,000 in retirement money to stay the course and last the rest of your life. Most people simply do not have that kind of retirement savings.

AFHs offer an alternative that is kinder, more affordable, and more socially conscious. These small, locally operated, home-like facilities provide higher quality of care and living satisfaction. They have personal relationships with Operators and caregivers who know their individual needs and preferences. They are given 24/7 surveillance by caregivers who can recognize troublesome signs early and take appropriate action. This family-style environment offers companionship with other residents, who often share life experiences and cultures. For many seniors, their AFH is located in the same neighborhood, if it is not actually their converted family home. Among the many benefits of staying in the same locale are being close to family, shopping at familiar stores, going to established doctors, visiting with neighbors they've known for years, and enjoying beautiful gardens and sitting areas at the home.

Since AFHs are designed to provide higher levels of care as residents age and their health care needs increase, one huge benefit is being able to remain in the same facility. Little can be more disorienting for elders than having to transfer to a new, strange facility as they become more debilitated. For the social impact investor, this humane treatment is very important.

Businesses looking ahead to provide post-retirement care for employees might be interested in investing in AFHs. Perhaps the greatest retirement benefit is having a plan for long-term housing and care that will continue meeting needs as retirees age and keep

> Changes in environment, health, social situation, and other elements have a detrimental effect on senior wellbeing. This is especially well-understood in those with dementia. The resident has a decrease in overall functioning and worsening of overall health that does not return to their baseline status before the event.
> —Dr. Morris

them in the local community. Churches or religious groups may want to offer this type of personalized and humane care option to their aging members. AFHs are excellent vehicles for creating a community of like-minded people who share ethnic and cultural backgrounds. Living in a home among a small group who share familiar customs, food, and cultural outlooks can be a very rewarding experience for elders.

Another factor that appeals to the social impact investor is the contribution AFHs make to the local community economy. When an AFH goes up in a neighborhood, local businesses benefit from the revenue it drives toward them. The senior residents can keep their local doctors, bankers, hairdressers, manicurists, and visit the same barista who always adds that extra dash of cinnamon in their coffee. Many of the employees of the AFH are from nearby areas, given opportunities to earn a good living, and will also spend in the local economy. Caregivers often are single mothers from all walks of life who can now provide for their families in their local community, giving them a bright future they had no access to before. Yard maintenance crew, cleaning staff, suppliers, and others find employment at the AFH.

Carbon footprint is another consideration for the social impact investor. When an AFH goes up in a neighborhood, the carbon footprint is kept as small as possible. Driving times for family, relatives, and employees are less since they are located in the area. Gardens with trees and green shrubs add oxygen to the atmosphere to offset carbon dioxide. Solar panels are often installed for more environmental benefit.

> "The warrior, for us, is one who sacrifices himself for the good of others. His task is to take care of the elderly, the defenseless, those who cannot provide for themselves. . ."
> —Sitting Bull, Lakota Chief

Existing structures are preferred and modified to meet regulations, rather than starting new construction. Compare these to the huge carbon footprint of a large corporate-run institutional assisted living facility.

Many people are willing to donate to good causes, which is essentially investing in causes that are meaningful and helpful to others. We call this "doing good," "giving back," and "paying it forward." What makes the model of the Adult Family Home an especially good fit for the socially minded investor is how it meets the Triple Bottom Line: AFH is a good product, with good profits, and for a good cause. It responds to the rapidly growing need to take good care of our elders.

Family Steward-Legacy Investor

Being a good steward of family finances and resources is an important value for investors in this group. Within this concept of stewardship is providing for the needs of aging parents and relatives. The family steward wants to find the best situation for Mom and Dad within budget requirements, and also preserve family assets as best as possible. Usually when parents reach the point of needing assistance with living that cannot be met within their current home, it falls to one or two adult children to take on the responsibility of figuring out what to do. This is a difficult time and too often fraught with conflict within the family. Aging parents can be resistant to change, even though they might admit that staying in the current home is risky and unworkable.

> "Religion that God our Father accepts as pure and faultless is this: to look after orphans and widows in their distress..."
> —Book of James

Various adult children may see the situation differently, some not believing change is needed, others disagreeing on what action to take. When such family conflicts arise, it's helpful to have an experienced management company to provide expert guidance and mediation, such as MyAFH. Benefits of a management company will be discussed in the next chapter.

As we noted before, many people do not know of better alternatives than assisted living facilities. Monthly rentals for rooms in ALFs can run upward of $4,000 to $5,000, which is a huge financial drain for most families. If extra services are needed, these can easily double the cost, depending on level of care. Those who are unprepared for facing long-term assisted living care for themselves or elderly parents may be thrown into crisis, feeling confused and frantic about what to do. In some cases, elderly couples are being counseled to file for a divorce in order to shift existing resources to the healthier spouse. The ailing spouse then becomes "destitute" and therefore eligible for Medicaid-paid assisted living. Another variation on this tactic is for families to hide financial resources behind the veil of a trust. This process appears to accomplish the spending down of assets required by Medicaid by shifting

> "A population that does not take care of the elderly and of children and the young has no future, because it abuses both its memory and its promise."
> —Francis of Assisi

them to other family members. In order to qualify for federal and state assistance through Medicaid, the senior must be shown to possess low enough financial assets to rate below poverty level.

While these tactics are technically legal, they border on being unethical by exploiting a system meant to serve the truly poor. Another factor to consider is that the higher quality ALFs have few or no Medicaid beds, forcing the senior to live in a sub-par facility. Staged divorces and trusts with ulterior motives often lead to alienation and animosity among spouses and family members. Keeping families together and mutually supportive is a better goal for promoting health in the final years of life.

Rather than simply paying several thousand dollars each month for assisted living (ALF), where elders most likely will not receive the best quality of care, investing that money into an adult family home (AFH) offers a great option. Once an AFH for Mom and Dad is on the radar, the family steward leads the way toward converting the parents' home, or purchasing a different residential property for an AFH. There are several approaches to creating an AFH, as previously discussed. The stewards could build an Accessory Dwelling Unit (ADU) on the property for themselves or other family members to live in. The stewards could become Owner/Operators or they could lease the home to an AFH Operator. If so inclined, they could even take part in caregiving.

Instead of watching thousands of dollars flowing out each month for assisted living care, the stewards will have created the mechanism for thousands of dollars to flow back each month. This positive cash flow can continue as long as the AFH is operating. It becomes an increasingly valuable piece of real estate that can be passed down as an inheritance. The funds generated from this investment can aid the family in many ways, such as paying for college, making down payments on homes, and taking vacations. The stewards are building a sustainable nest egg for future generations that can last many years. They are creating a valuable family legacy. Extended family can also take part in this endeavor. As grandchildren grow into young adults, the field of caregiving is a great place to start their work experience.

The family steward investor thus preserves assets rather than spending them down. This sets up wealth for generations. It sets up a safety net for future retirement and long-term care in advance, waiting until the need arises in the family. What could be better financial stewardship than creating such a ripple effect through the family and into the future? It's not only being a good, caring child but also a good steward in the fullest sense of the word—one who creates a valuable family legacy for generations.

Calculating Return on Investment (ROI) for an Adult Family Home

One of the first questions that a savvy investor will ask is, "What is my ROI for this investment?" ROI (Return on Investment) is a measure of performance used to evaluate the efficiency of an investment. ROI is calculated by subtracting the initial value of the investment from its final value, which is equal to the net return, and then dividing the net return by the cost of the investment. This number is multiplied by 100 to obtain the ROI. For example, if you had a net return of $30,000 and your investment cost you $20,000, your ROI is 0.5 (or 50%).

FINAL VALUE — COST OF INVESTMENT ÷ COST OF INVESTMENT = R.O.I.

In calculating the ROI for AFHs, several factors enter the equation. There is the value of an existing property or the cost of acquiring a suitable new property. Then there are the renovation and construction expenses to bring the house and grounds into compliance with the numerous regulations for Adult Family Homes. Usually, at least 3-4 additional bedrooms must be added for a total of 8 bedrooms for residents. Living space, including bedroom and bathroom, must be constructed for the person who oversees day-to-day operations. This might be a Resident Manager, or the Operator and Owner. Many Investors choose to add an Accessory Dwelling Unit (ADU) of around 700-800 square feet to the property for themselves or other family members. Most AFHs are at least 3,000 square feet in size. Remodeling the current square footage of the house will cost about $125 per square foot, and building additional space will cost about $200 per square foot.

Case Study: PC Family

The PC family had several considerations when they made the decision to invest in an Adult Family Home. They wanted to make sound financial choices and be good stewards of family assets while also providing a continuing source of compassionate housing and living assistance for their aging mother. Their mother's family home, where she was currently living after her husband's death, was not ideal for an increasingly frail senior. The family was losing $2,500 per month trying to keep up the house and grounds and provide the care their mother needed. The daughters were spending a lot of time trying to manage the household and their mother's needs, which took them away from their own homes and families. Their mother felt isolated and had few activities or friends. They were worried about having to place their mother in a nursing home and possibly having to get her on welfare and Medicaid due to shrinking monetary resources.

After several meetings with the staff of an AFH management company, the daughters decided to proceed with converting the family home into an AFH. The property was valued at $500,000 when they began the process. It needed remodeling and adding several bedrooms, and they opted to build an ADU. The upstairs could be used for the Resident Manager, who needed a place to stay on-site. The cost of remodeling the home and grounds to state specifications for an AFH was $450,000. The management company assisted with finding qualified staff and advertising to attract residents. Once renovations and additions were completed, and the bedrooms were filled, the cash flow improved considerably, and the AFH started operating at a profit. The lease agreement between the AFH and the PC family resulted in a monthly net profit for the PC family of $2.500. Putting together the monthly profit plus removing the $2,500 monthly loss ($5,000 combined), the family was essentially netting $60,000 income per year.

The PC family was grateful that within a short two-year time period, they were able to turn around their financial situation and replace the family's $2,500 monthly loss with the same level in profit. They now had a stable income source that provided financial security for their mother and other family members well into the future. Perhaps best of all, they no longer had to worry about their mother's wellbeing, about where they would get care for her, and how much longer the money would hold out. Mom had activities whenever she wanted, a group of companions, and felt reassured that she would not become a burden to the family. Instead, she knew her property was helping the family make money, and she felt happy and useful watching over the new family business.

Calculating the ROI for the PC Family

Calculated over a period of two years, the PC Family made a substantial return on investment by converting their family home into an AFH. Taking the original property value of $500,000 and adding $450,000 remodeling costs, the total cost of investment was $950,000. Within a two-year period, the value of their property increased to $1,300,000, which is the gain of their investment (based upon bank appraisal). Calculations of ROI using the formula are quite good: **36.84% ROI.**

GAIN OF INVESTMENT	COST OF INVESTMENT	COST OF INVESTMENT	R.O.I.
$1,300,000.00	$950,000.00	$950,000.00	36.84%

Case Study: JD Family

The story of JD and her family provides a different view into how investors in AFHs can make a difference in the lives of other people. In particular, the story speaks to social impact investors. JD came to the U.S. from the Philippines with her two children, pregnant with the third. Initially, she worked providing child care for her sister, but realized she needed a more reliable and better-paying career.

She studied to become a caregiver and found employment, but still could not make ends meet. After sending her children back to the Philippines to stay with family, she faced a divorce and never received child support, working two jobs with only a half-day off each week, but still living paycheck to paycheck.

After working for several years as a caregiver, JD gained considerable experience and followed her sister's suggestion that she seek work as a Resident Manager at an AFH management company. She felt capable of managing caregiver staff and helping them grow toward success. When she learned that she could move into an AFH home as a manager with her three children and not pay rent—*and* earn a good salary—she was overjoyed. Now she did not need to work multiple jobs and could focus on her roles with the AFH staff and residents and her children. Supported and mentored by the AFH management company, JD learned more about the business and their vision for the future of their employees. Soon she was advanced to become an Operator for one of their Adult Family Homes and felt equipped to fulfill these additional responsibilities. With an increased salary, JD was able to not only provide for her children's needs, but also some of their wants. She believes this is one of the greatest blessings in her life, giving her direction and a solid career, and giving her children a bright future.

Are You Ready for the Next Step?

Hopefully, it is abundantly clear that investing in Adult Family Homes is an outstanding opportunity for you, whether you are a real estate investor, social impact investor, or family steward-legacy investor. Your ability to make considerable profits in a relatively short time period is excellent, whether you want to have one AFH or would like to own multiple AFHs. Naturally, taking on multiple AFHs will increase the workload and logistics, which would need careful planning. To operate successful homes, you will need additional staff, food, cleaning supplies, yard maintenance, and suppliers for appliances and materials. Another thing that becomes challenging is keeping the rooms filled; the target is to have 95% occupancy. Most Owners find they need a secure relationship with referral agents and sophisticated, targeted advertising. This is where partnering with an AFH management company offers many advantages to help you attain a successful and profitable business.

The next chapter addresses the "do it yourself" approach versus joining forces with a management company such as MyAFH. You may be surprised at how many details and widespread factors come into play when setting up an AFH. With MyAFH remodeling or building and managing your home for you, this could save you thousands if not tens of thousands of dollars in potential mistakes. Especially if you have not done something like this before, the expertise that MyAFH brings could give you huge savings in such things as change orders and construction cost overruns.

You can involve a management company as little or as much as you want. This can be anything from a small investment for them to evaluate the suitability of your home, to having the company guide you through every phase of the project to make certain that everything is done right.

So, take the next steps to forge ahead and consider if you have what it takes to do it alone, or if having an expert management company ready at hand is best for you.

4

DO I HAVE WHAT IT TAKES?

NOW THAT YOU'VE decided to become an investor in Adult Family Homes, it's time to take a closer look at the various routes and which one will work best for you. This is a big decision, but don't worry—there is help! Experts at AFH management companies can assist you with the myriad of things to consider as you approach the tasks involved in creating and managing an AFH. Even though there are numerous requirements and several steps to accomplish, the goal of creating a desirable senior living home is well worth the effort. By keeping this goal in focus and organizing your approach, you can do it. If you need help, there are experienced advisors you can turn to for each phase of the process.

So, you are starting a business; do you have what it takes? You'll need to get involved in marketing, financing, operations, sales, human resources and employees, medical compliance, construction regulations, and legal requirements—either by doing the work yourself or having someone experienced and skilled to do it on your behalf. Perhaps the best option for finding this expertise in one place is seeking a reputable AFH management company.

While these are a lot of hats for one person or couple to wear, some of these hats will be worn by others, guided by your needs, abilities, and comfort levels. The others might include attorneys, real estate experts, government officials, banks, accountants, your staff, and a management company. Remember, there are also hundreds of state and federal regulations that Adult Family Homes must meet. Washington State, which is used as the main example, is the most highly regulated for AFH compliance, with over 700 regulations to be aware of and meet. Even with these challenges, it is still a great opportunity that is well within your reach.

As mentioned at the end of the previous chapter, if you don't have experience in running an Adult Family Home, you could cost yourself many thousands of dollars by making mistakes. Every regulation you have not met will lead to costly additions, remodels, fines, and lost revenue. Not to mention the emotional stress of working through the consequences of unnecessary errors. Missteps could delay your opening for business and set your timeline in arrears. You might delay when your AFH business becomes a profitable enterprise by not passing the up-front compliance requirements in a timely manner. This could require you to sink more thousands of dollars into the operations.

Consider your choice carefully as you decide what your level of involvement in creating and operating your AFH will be. We call this "coming to TERMs" with your role. You will need to assess where you stand with each part.

TIME	**ENERGY**	**RESOURCES**	**MONEY**
Are you able to give copious amounts of time to this project?	Do you have abundant energy for long hours of work?	Do you have multiple contacts in various aspects of the AFH business?	Are your financial assets sufficient for necessary cash infusions?

Time

It takes a lot of time to assume responsibility for getting an AFH up and running. Because there are so many details and regulations, you'll need to study documents and consult with experts, such as attorneys and experienced AFH managers. You'll need to deal with government agencies regarding structural and safety requirements for the house and medical regulations for the care of residents. There could be considerable back and forth as you weave your way through these bureaucracies. Then you must deal with city building codes and requirements, navigating their bureaucracy and time-lines. Once you've got the construction process underway, you need to plan for hiring employees and attracting residents. Marketing becomes a critical factor, and this is a specialized field. If you have a job, these time requirements may simply be unrealistic. You must also take into consideration the impact that devoting so much time to the AFH project will have on your family.

Energy

Continually staying on top of so many moving parts will require a large amount of energy. Here is where you must make a candid assessment of how much energy you can give to this AFH project. If you're in great health and good physical shape, you will have a lot of energy to give. If not, trying to take charge of the AFH project may be extremely taxing of your energy. It would be a sad outcome if you damaged your own health while in the process of providing a comfortable and caring long-term housing option for your parents and/or other residents.

Another aspect to consider in this area of energy is the extent of your talents and skill sets. It's only fair to ask yourself how good you are with each of the essentials of running a successful business that were mentioned in the opening paragraph of this section, especially the "Big 3" of marketing/sales, day-to-day management, and operations and staffing.

With marketing, there is the constant, never-ceasing work of getting seen out there in the type of business in which you compete. This brings into play what the "other guys" are doing to capture that same prospective resident you need to keep your beds full. How do you differentiate your offering from theirs and do a better job of delivering on your promises? How many leads do you need to generate each month for your salespeople (or yourself) to work with in order to convert enough prospects into clients? Where do those leads come from? How much does it cost to generate good leads? What is the closing ratio of your salesperson, or yourself? All of this type of activity is aimed at one thing crucial to the success of an Adult Family Home—that of keeping the beds filled.

When you are managing operations, your eyes and hands are on the controls, ensuring that all the people and systems actually work together to get the job done. In this case, the job is assuring quality care for your residents while meeting the state's record-keeping compliance requirements. Obviously, there is necessary training for all job categories if things are going to be done the right way.

One of the most challenging aspects of staffing for Adult Family Homes is that of finding and retaining competent and compassionate caregivers. These are the front-line people who will either make or break the business in terms of delivering on the experience you have promised families in your marketing and sales efforts. How good are you at hiring and firing? Have you had human resource experience? Do you work well with minority and/or immigrant populations who may not completely understand your language and customs? Do your employees share your same goal of quality and safety; do they have the motivation to work in this field like you do?

You can see that the big issue of on-going compliance depends on how well your staff executes their responsibilities. Getting cited for compliance violations during the regular, frequent check-ins the state performs carries with it the threat of having your business shut down for a time, or even losing your license to operate an Adult Family Home (now or in the future). And, of course, if you have to shut your doors for a time, you are not making money. In fact, you may be losing money. Thus, the amount of talent, skills, and energy you have and are willing to invest is the fuel that will drive the success of your Adult Family Home. Because energy demands are so high in this business, many Owner/Operators wisely partner with seasoned veterans such as MyAFH to bring what is required to the table.

It is common for existing Adult Family Home Owner/Operators who have been at it for as few as a couple of years, or as many as several decades, to reach the point where they feel overtaxed. There will be those good folks who, for various reasons, say, "It's time for me to get out." They may have all the compassion needed, but then there is the day-to-day competency and commitment needed to run a business and still have time for themselves and family. In this type of scenario, MyAFH can either bring resources to the table for the Owner via service contracts, or purchase the business and real estate from existing Owner/Operators.

Resources

Some people have multiple connections in the health care or construction industries, and can turn to these associates for resources. Others may not have such networks, so their resources are limited. You'll need to assess where you stand in terms of resources, experienced friends, or associates who can offer advice and assistance. When looking at resources, also think of connections in such businesses as marketing, employment, landscaping, home decoration, legal advice, and financial experts. If you don't have a wide range of such resources, you may be getting in over your head if you try to do the project on your own.

One way to quickly bring needed resources on board is to team up with an AFH management company. Most companies have the specialists on staff to guide you through each step in the regulatory, legal, construction, and personnel management processes. You might not need help in every area, so you have options to select which experts fit your needs.

Below is an example of the staff of a typical AFH management company, where you can see the areas of expertise within their organization.

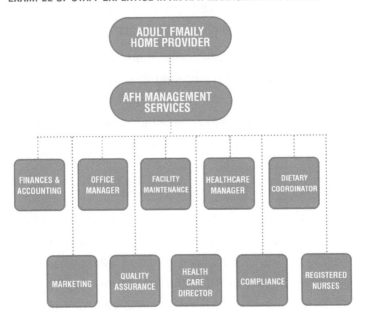

Money

They say money is the bottom line for carrying out any project. While there are many approaches to creative financing, you'll need to carefully consider what monetary resources you have to invest in your AFH. Where are your sources of investment capital, should you need these? Financing the construction and operation of an AFH is often beyond the monetary capacity of an individual. Although it should be clear that operating an AFH can be a very profitable business, you still need to invest a considerable sum in getting it going. You may want to consider a small business, residential real estate, or bridge loan for operating capital.

Other options to consider regarding finances would include partnering with an existing AFH management company or becoming part of an established franchise model operating in the adult family home arena.(For more in-depth discussion regarding franchise opportunities see the section on franchising at the end of this chapter.)

The franchise model is becoming more common for finding a suitable location for an AFH, securing financing, and assistance in successfully operating a home. Franchising makes a lot of sense in this particular industry in which systems, processes, and discipline have always been the "Achilles heel" for Owner/Operators. This franchise model is also an option available through MyAFH.

In light of the above considerations, the basic choices before you are to "go it alone," to partner with an AFH management company (such as MyAFH) or to become involved in a franchise operation. If you choose to have a management company partner, then you have choices about how much assistance you want from them. With MyAFH, for instance, you can have a wide range of assistance, everything from simply evaluating your home for suitability to partnering in every phase of the project. Within this range, there are many options for how involved you want MyAFH to be, and these can be negotiated and changed. It all depends upon what level of involvement you choose for yourself.

Several factors will affect your financial requirements for opening and operating an AFH. The chart below shows the best estimate by MyAFH for initial expenses in establishing and operating your AFH. Your actual costs may be greater or less than these estimates, depending upon the location of your property and current relevant market conditions. Costs will also be influenced by your management capabilities, local economic conditions, and how quickly your AFH reaches capacity.

FIRST 12 MONTHS AFH START-UP INVESTMENT

YOUR ESTIMATED INITIAL INVESTMENT

EXPENDITURES	AMOUNT	
	LOW	HIGH
Travel, Lodging, Meals, etc. for initial training	$1,500	$2,000
Land, Building, & Renovation (1)	$500,000	$1,000,000
Utilities	$1,800	$2,100
Licenses & Permits	$4,000	$7,500
Printing, Signage	$1,000	$2,000
Furniture & Equipment	$35,000	$75,000
Initial Advertising Expenses (including Grand Opening)	$10,000	$10,000
Insurance	$2,500	$5,000
Opening Inventory	$25,000	$35,000
Materials & Supplies	$2,000	$3,000
Professional Fees (2)	$750	$3,500
Computer Equipment & Software	$7,000	$12,000
Telephone System, Internet & Cable Service	$1,200	$4,000
Additional Funds for 12 Months (3)	$25,000	$50,000
TOTAL ESTIMATED INITIAL INVESTMENT (12)	$616,750	$1,211,150

Notes:

(1) The costs associated with land, building and renovations vary greatly depending upon your AFH location and size of the building, number of bedrooms and baths, finish levels and amenities.

(2) You may incur legal fees, accounting fees and other professional fees in order to incorporate your business, perform all necessary tax filings and to set up a small business including a general ledger, tax reports, payroll deposits, etc.

(3) The estimate of additional funds is based on an owner-operated business and does not include any allowance for an owner's draw. The estimate is for a period of twelve months. In general, you may expect to put additional cash into the business during at least the first twelve (12) months.

(4) These estimated initial expenses are our best estimate of the costs you may incur in establishing and operating your AFH. We have relied on our experience in this industry in compiling these estimates. Your actual costs will depend on several management and economic factors. You should review these figures carefully with a business advisor before making any decision to purchase an AFH.

Choosing Your Level of Involvement

The previous chapter described these three types of AFH investors: Real estate investor, social impact investor, and family steward/ legacy investor. These definitions are based upon the investor's motivations and goals for becoming involved in an AFH. This section takes a different approach and examines investors from another perspective—that of their chosen level of involvement in AFH operations. This involvement can range from purely investing money in the AFH real estate market to varying amounts of direct participation in running the AFH.

There are three levels of involvement that you might select: Real estate Owner only, real estate Owner and AFH business Operator, and AFH business Operator only. If you choose to be only a real estate Owner, you'll need to find someone to run your AFH. If you decide to be only an Operator of an AFH, you'll need to pair with someone who is the real estate Owner. Or, you could choose to be an Owner/Operator and be involved in all aspects of the AFH business. Relationships between the investor and the AFH Operators are crucial to a successful business operation. The graphic below illustrates the types of people who often become Operators, and the common sources for AFH investors.

Each of the three levels of involvement for an AFH investor has particular pros and cons. In the next section, scenarios for each level of involvement are described to elaborate on the advantages and drawbacks of each.

Scenario 1: Real Estate Owner

This is an ideal situation for someone who wants to be involved in the Adult Family Home arena but has no inclination or motive to participate in the day-to-day business operations. The real estate investor/owner approaches this just like any other type of real estate investment they may be considering. How attractive is this particular location, and is the region growing? How long before this residential facility starts producing positive cash flow? How much might the carrying costs be? What kind of ROI (Return On Investment) are these types of properties historically generating? What is the chance of this property appreciating in value? How hard will it be to find and keep good, long-term tenants?

Adult Family Homes shine as real estate investments in all of these areas. As an Owner, you are able to sign a long-term lease with a reputable Adult Family Home operator for a higher monthly rate when compared to renting it to a simple residential user, such as an individual or family. Many of the hassles faced by landlords are reduced, such as finding good tenants, maintaining the building and landscaping, and dealing with unexpected emergencies.

Qualified AFH Operators are prepared to handle these things effectively. Operators assume responsibility for credentialing and compliance with state requirements and all aspects of running the AFH business. The AFH business Owner/Operator pays the mortgage while you, the real estate owner, receive monthly lease payments established contractually, typically for longer lease terms than are standard practice for single family residential real estate. For example, a typical lease contract for a residential adult family home would be for 5 years minimum, with options for additional 5-year renewals. You can see the great value here as a real estate owner of not being subject to such negative cost factors as vacancies and tenant turnover. Not to mention how lenders, such as banks, place higher value on reliable revenue streams in calculating their loan commitments.

What kind long-term lease contract could you as the real estate owner expect to enter into with an adult family home business Owner/Operator? Typically, Owner/Operators will pay within a range of $750-$1500 per bed, depending on factors such as the local market, neighborhood, home condition, and street appeal. So, for a 6-bedroom Adult Family Home that would translate to anywhere between $4,500-$9,000 per month in revenue to you, the real estate owner. For a single-family residence set up for 6 bedrooms/3 baths, these lease amounts usually far exceed what that home would rent for as a single-family home.

Finding the right person to lease the property and operate the AFH is the biggest challenge for the real estate owner. This is not an easy process. The AFH business Owner and Operator must be trustworthy and responsible, qualified and experienced in running this type of business, and someone with whom the real estate owner can work well. Although day-to-day operations are done by the AFH business, the real estate owner is wise to keep track of how things are going. Otherwise, they may face a rude awakening when regulators assess fines for non-compliance or the business fails due to insolvency. Partnering with an AFH management company can relieve the real estate owner of this oversight responsibility and protect against failure to comply with regulations or poor business practices.

The option of being a real estate owner is something a family could consider when they have a suitable property and do not want to operate an AFH business. If they are facing the prospect of placing a loved one in an assisted living situation, this becomes even more appealing. When you or the family own the real estate and one of the bedrooms is occupied by your loved one, you actually may cover the cost of this assisted living care for the rest of the loved one's life through income from other beds in the AFH. Using family resources in this manner becomes part of the concept of what it means to be a good steward of family finances.

Real estate owners generally do not wish to participate in taking care of residents; for some, this is a drawback, but others may prefer it. Sometimes the real estate owner knows someone, such as a retired nurse, who they could tap to fill the Operator role. If you have such a person, that could be a great "partnership". If you don't, then that's where a seasoned operator like MyAFH can step in, either in the position of management company or franchisor.

Scenario 2: Operator

This is an ideal situation for the person who has the training and experience to successfully run an Adult Family Home business on a day-to-day basis but does not have the financial means to secure and renovate a good residential property in a desirable market area. In partnering with a real estate owner, the Operator brings to the table the elements that the real estate owner is seeking: someone who is qualified to run the AFH business and will enter a long-term lease at above the market rate. Over time, these two parties may work out other levels of revenue and/or equity sharing. The key in all this is the competent Operator. This is where MyAFH can be an effective resource with its rigorous selection, training, and systems approach to creating successful Operators.

Operators control and run the AFH business, and can get assistance by involving their own family in various aspects. Family members can provide a base of support for the Operator, usually contributing to the success of the business. For many people, providing direct care to residents is a source of satisfaction. Operators and their caregiving staff are in face to face contact with residents of the AFH and their families. Direct feedback from residents and their families helps the Operator ensure that goals and standards for care are met.

The Operator must obtain all the state certifications and credentials necessary for running an AFH, meet compliance requirements, and make sure the staff is qualified. All the supervisory responsibilities rest upon the Operator, who puts a great deal of time and energy into the business. For some, these demands may become overwhelming. Having help from the Operator's family members can alleviate some of this pressure. From a financial point of view, because the Operator is leasing the business the monthly lease payment is an outflow of money. If the AFH keeps its beds at capacity and operates efficiently, there will be adequate inflow of money to generate sufficient profits for making a good living.

The real estate Owner (who owns the house and property and leases these to the Operator) has financial responsibility for maintenance of the property, including repairs and improvements. Owners who avoid or delay necessary maintenance and repairs can subject the AFH business to the actions of regulators, who check on compliance regularly and could assess fines or even close the business for serious violations.

The critical factor for the Operator is teaming up with a reliable and trustworthy real estate Owner. This is not an easy process, since there are real estate Owners who care primarily about making a profit on their investment and are not concerned about the quality of care and soundness of the AFH business. They may cut corners and use inferior materials to increase profits, leading to mistakes and oversights causing violations of state requirements. AFH management companies such as MyAFH can avoid such pitfalls and facilitate successful businesses by matching competent Operators with reliable Owners.

Scenario 3: Real Estate Owner and Operator

There are many advantages when the same person is both the real estate Owner and Operator of an AFH business. Previous sections covered the issues and challenges that individuals or families face when taking on all the responsibilities and risks associated with having complete control over an Adult Family Home business. With higher responsibilities and risks also come higher rewards, both in terms of meaningful work and dollars. Of course, that is true with most business ventures. But there is one key consideration when evaluating a business opportunity that makes the Adult Family Home business a current standout. Market supply and demand will continue to rise for assisted living senior care, which was covered in the section on demographic and socioeconomic statistics earlier in this book. The dynamics of the marketplace have worked in favor of those Owner/Operators who have been willing to get the right training and consistently apply the right systems in building their businesses.

Since the Owner/Operator has full control over all aspects of the AFH business, it's easier to make sure everything is being run properly and efficiently. Direct feedback from residents and families helps ensure that problems are identified early and solutions found, so that care standards are met. This close contact facilitates a sound, caring, and successful senior care business.

If you choose to be an Operator of an AFH, you will be closely connected with caregiving and have face to face contact with residents and their families. You may decide to be a caregiver yourself, or you may hire staff and be responsible for supervising the caregivers. Many times, the caregivers are members of your family. They will be taking care of the most vulnerable members of society who are elderly or have disabling conditions, including some with challenging behaviors, physical and developmental disabilities, mental illness, and limiting medical conditions. It's important that you and your family feel committed to serving this vulnerable population, and have the ability to meet their needs with kindness and compassion.

While being an AFH Owner/Operator can be a rewarding experience, it is also very tiring and stressful work. It may be harder to maintain boundaries between work and family life, especially when family members are involved in the business. Being available to residents day and night, week in and week out, can be draining. Someone must be awake on the premises to oversee and respond to residents' needs all through the night. You may decide to hire staff to fulfill this overnight supervision role.

Another challenging aspect of senior care is the inevitable decline and death of your residents. Some Operators and caregivers find it difficult to watch people they have come to know and care about go through their final days. Although the process usually occurs over many years, there will be a continuous experience of bonding with residents and then losing them. It's important that you and your family have adequate support structures to bolster you through these experiences.

As a licensed AFH Owner/Operator, you assume responsibilities that could have an enormous impact on both you and your family. There is the constant necessity to meet and remain in compliance with numerous regulations involving both the property and the care of residents. The greatest amount of oversight comes from the State's Department of Social and Health Services or comparable state agency, tasked with protecting the safety of vulnerable elderly and disabled people. This requires frequent monitoring of daily caregiving activities as well as safety and structural conditions of the facilities. You want to make sure that your AFH operation is always in compliance with these regulations. This prevents you from receiving citations, fines, enforcements, or ultimately being shut down. While it takes effort to comply with regulations, remember that these government agencies are here to protect residents, not to harm your business.

> Many people in the medical field believe it is a privilege to be with patients and families at the end of life. When someone passes, those present feel involved in a spiritual event. Like birth, death connects us with the unknown and the mystery, illuminating a bigger picture of life. This act of kindness, guiding a family through the loss of a loved one, is both sad and joyous—one of the most rewarding things you will ever do.
> —Dr. Morris

Operating an AFH and being involved in caregiving is a major commitment. Making this choice calls for someone who truly cares for the well-being of others. Operators who are in the business simply to make lots of money are rarely successful--their lack of compassion will be reflected in reduced quality of care, which will affect reputation and ability to attract future residents. Operators who enter the AFH business with the main focus on giving compassionate care to residents, and who follow good business ethics will almost always be successful.

LEVELS OF INVOLVEMENT	✔ PROS	✘ CONS
Real Estate Owner	No need to get credentialed	Cap on monthly payment at full occupancy
	Mortgage paid by AFH Owner	Lower payments with fewer residents
	Guaranteed lease payment each month	Takes up time find a qualified AFH Operator
	Additional payments based on occupancy	Unable to participate in care of residents
Real Estate Owner & Operator	Make long term real estate investment	Responsible for both house and AFH business credentials
	Continured income	
	Greatest opportunity for growth	Inadequate planning leads to being overwhelmed
	More lines of revenue	Harder to keep boundaries between work & family
	Enrich your skills as you contribute to your business	Demanding workload
Operator	Financial responsibility for house upkeep falls on owner	Must obtain credentials
	You control AFH business operations	Paying monthly lease is outflow of profits
	Family support/involvement can benefit all	Time investment running business may be overwhelming
	Direct care of residents is satisfying	Must find responsible and trustworthy owner

LEVELS OF AFH INVOLVEMENT
PROS & CONS

What Kind of Involvement Fits For You?

Take an honest look at these three types of involvement with operating an AFH business. Decide which fits best for you, according to your goals and motivations.

Real Estate Owner: I am interested in the business aspects of AFHs and want to invest in property that has high potential for a good ROI. I have looked into AFHs and believe they offer excellent business opportunities. I am not inclined to enter day-to-day operations of an AFH.

"As a **Real Estate Owner**... I'm interested in **achieving a higher return** on my investment as compared with typical residential or commercial leased properties."

"As an **AFH Operator**... I'm looking for opportunities to expand my skills and abilities so I can both **Do Well** (make a good living) and **Do Good** (benefit elders who typically are served by government and/or non-profit organizations."

Operator: I am drawn to being involved in running senior living facilities that provide home-like, compassionate, and quality care. My experiences and background give me a sound base to become an Operator, but I don't presently have the financial capacity to become an Owner.

Real Estate Owner/Operator: I want to be immersed in the day-to-day care, operations, and business aspects of AFHs. I feel drawn to the senior care and housing sector, have suitable experience and background, and have the ability to become an AFH Owner.

"As an **owner/operator...** I enjoy the responsibility of running all aspects of an AFH business that **ensures both the welfare of my aging parents, but also enhances the family estate** being passed on to future generations."

The Case of Marco (Real Estate Owner)

Marco* is experienced with investing in Real Estate. He has owned a few single-family homes in the area. After several years of dealing with the ups and downs of renting his homes to families, he was looking at possibly purchasing commercial real estate, which has a greater initial investment yet a potential for greater return. He researched a few opportunities that would be available, then, through a mutual friend, he was introduced to the Adult Family Home senior care industry and MyAFH. Marco's knowledge of real estate helped him see the benefits of being involved with this type of business.

His biggest hesitation in jumping into this venture was the thought of having to deal with elderly people in need of care. His family is stable and not looking to change careers in order to operate a home. Marco was not interested in adding the credentials needed to become an Operator, but he could see the long-term benefits and profitability of leasing real estate to an AFH business. It took some time working with MyAFH to get all his questions answered and feel confident about his role in the project. Eventually, he decided to move forward with purchasing property suitable for building and made plans to build up to three AFHs there. As the real estate property Owner, he is involved in the building plans and expenses, but not in operating the business. Someone at MyAFH will be handling the actual AFH business and overseeing the care of residents. Marco's involvement starts and stops at the building itself, which is what he desires. He appreciates the steady income and lower risk for long-term losses that this real estate investment brings.

The Case of Julie (Operator)

Julie* is a hardworking single mother who found herself in need of a stable career to better take care of her children. As a young adult, being a wife and mother was a full-time job that she found fulfilling, and she was very satisfied with her life. As happens when tragedy strikes, major changes overturned her life and she found herself needing to provide for her three children by herself. In a matter of weeks, Julie went through training to get her certification as a Home Care Aide and found employment with an agency for hourly work. Through these jobs she was able to gain substantial experience with different types of residents, level of care needs, and family dynamics. A few months later she took on additional jobs in order to make ends meet. She kept up this grueling pace for a few years, until her sister introduced her to MyAFH. With all her experience, dedication, compassion, and determination, the company quickly recognized her ability and she was advanced to become an AFH Resident Manager. At this better paid position she was finally financially able to focus on only one job. She was able to move into the ADU (Accessory Dwelling Unit) of the AFH, so now housing for her children, one of her biggest stressors, was no longer an issue.

Throughout Julie's time with MyAFH, she showed great knowledge and shared her expertise with others in the company. When the time came that a property was looking for an Operator to run the business, she was the best candidate for the position. With the support and guidance of her mentors at MyAFH, she was able to become a small business owner and operate her own AFH. Julie realizes that without their support, she would not have been able to own a business—not because she wasn't capable, but because she would not have realized it was an option and would not have known how to get started.

The Case of William
(Real Estate Owner and Operator)

William* is an example of a person who moved through various levels of involvement in the AFH business. His journey shows how commitment, right training, and systematic application of knowledge lead to success. In this unique situation, William was able to advance from being a caregiver to a Resident Manager, and then to a real estate Owner and AFH business Operator.

William came into the eco-system of MyAFH several years ago and has grown and prospered as a result. He immigrated to Washington State as a young, married family man from his home country of Kenya. His initial interaction with MyAFH was as a caregiver in one of the several Adult Family Homes they owned and operated at the time. Because of William's hard work over several years and desire to advance in the business, the owner of MyAFH promoted him to a Resident Manager position in one of their AFHs.

In time his abilities in this new position led to a partnership agreement which helped him become an Operator of one of the MyAFH homes.

At that time, William did not have the financial resources or credit to secure a real estate loan to become an Owner/Operator of an Adult Family Home. What he did have was the knowledge of systems, processes, and programs he learned and applied while working as a caregiver and later manager for MyAFH. As his abilities and experience expanded, the company recognized he was capable of being an AFH Operator. Soon, William was advanced into an AFH Operator position assuming full responsibility for running the business. Continuing to grow and apply what he had learned, he was successful as an Operator, and the higher pay strengthened his financial situation. After a few years functioning in the role and responsibilities of an Operator, William met with financial advisors and was able to parlay his earnings into the purchase of his own residential property, which he converted into an Adult Family Home. Now he is both the real estate Owner and the AFH business Operator.

Success with that endeavor enabled William and his family to purchase another home, this one as their own private residence in a bedroom community of Seattle, WA. Today, William has his sights set on launching his second Adult Family Home in the area. In all, William's is an impressive true story of how someone with drive can immigrate to this country with literally nothing and build their way into productive citizenship and financial success. The AFH business was an excellent vehicle for William to expand his skills and gain experience, setting a foundation for personal and business growth.

*Each case is a real example. The actual names have been changed.

FRANCHISE: Another Consideration

In looking at the three basic levels of involvement under consideration: real estate owner, business operator and real estate owner/business operator, any one, or all, can be accommodated under the concept of franchising. Franchising can be of great benefit, especially for those who are seeking existing expertise and effective systems when getting started.

It provides a proven pathway when creating your new AFH, whether you are modifying an existing house, buying a new property or taking over an already functioning AFH. The advantages of a franchise unit model include the benefits of the franchisor's design, marketing, staffing, construction, and financial, legal and operational systems. These are key business elements that have been tested and proven, versus setting out and creating by trial and error on your own.

MyAFH has the distinction in the senior care sector of being the first to offer the opportunity to join the network of their established operations. This comes through its affiliation with the national franchisor, AFH Senior Care Corporation, the licensing entity across the United States for individual Franchise Units and for geographic Regional Developers.

The franchise option is perhaps the best alternative for a successful investment in this burgeoning market of senior care. As John Naisbitt, the author of *Megatrends: Ten New Directions Transforming Our Lives*[1] states: *"Franchising is the single-most successful marketing strategy ever created."*

Naisbitt is truly onto something when one takes a look at the numbers: Even though franchising represents only 8% of retail business locations across the U.S., franchises do over 40% of the total retail dollar volume. Add to that the fact that franchisers experience a 92% SUCCESS rate overall! Compare that with the FAILURE rate of most retail businesses. Why is this the reality? It's due to the brand name recognition, tested systems and proven support the franchising offers.

In the case of the above-mentioned franchisor, AFH Senior Care Corporation, the United States has been divided into 500 Regional Areas for development. Each region will support a minimum of 25 Franchise Units / Regional Area. A Regional Area consists of a population density of at least 250,000 people. Multiple Franchise Units may be owned by one individual or group.

An Area Developer (AD) in the AFH Senior Care system is an entrepreneur / business person who purchases the exclusive rights to a 250,000 person territory. The AD recruits new franchisees and helps them open their locations in his/her exclusive territory, following an agreed-upon schedule. The AD is trained by the Franchisor in how to perform the various services being provided to unit franchisees. The AD typically opens a pilot unit, hires a manager to operate it, and uses the pilot unit as a showcase in the local market for prospective unit franchisees.

It is the AD's responsibility to place franchisees in their area, assist the franchisees in finding a location and negotiating a lease, and providing opening assistance, training and support. In return for providing these services the AD profits from the initial franchise fee and royalty shares.

Financial considerations for both Franchise Units and Regional Developer in terms of investment requirements, revenue structures and potential returns are detailed for interested parties at: AFHSeniorCare.com/franchise

Taking Your Next Step

By this point, you have probably made an assessment of where you stand on TERM—Time, Energy, Resources, and Money—in regard to being in the AFH business. You've decided whether you can "go it alone," partner with an AFH management company or become a franchisee. Taking both the advantages and disadvantages of each level of involvement into consideration, you've settled on which one fits best for you.

Now it's time for you to take the next step. You will need to evaluate the property that you have in mind for creating your AFH. Is this property your home or a family home, another house that you want to convert, or will it be new construction? Assuming that you've chosen to partner with an AFH management company, what is the best type of relationship for your purposes? All these points will be covered in the next chapter.

5

IS MY PROPERTY RIGHT FOR AN AFH?

AT THIS POINT, you've concluded that becoming involved in the Adult Family Home business is a good fit for your particular situation. Congratulations! You may be approaching the next step as a Real Estate Owner, as an Operator of an AFH business, or as Owner-Operator moving toward full involvement. You may be motivated by the potential to realize a good ROI in real estate, or because you value the social impact of compassionate elder care and like-minded communities, or because you desire to be a good steward of family resources and create a legacy.

This diagram shows three options for being involved in the Adult Family Home business.

The immediate question for most people becomes: "Is the property that I, or my parents, my family, or my partners currently own or control a good one for launching a successful Adult Family Home business?" The proverbial answer is: "That depends."

It depends on two major considerations—location and ease of convertibility. The process of examining these considerations is reasonably straightforward. You must determine if the location of your property and suitability for conversion into an AFH will work. If not, you will be better served by securing a more suitable property elsewhere.

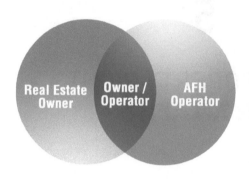

First, consider the issue of convertibility. Keep in mind that the remodeled AFH facility should have a minimum of five bedrooms (more if your state allows it), three or more bathrooms on the first level, and living space for a caregiver or residential manager. This living space could be on the second floor, and you could also have second-floor bedrooms for residents. However, second-floor rooms are required by fire codes to have access to exterior stairs or ramps in case of emergency. Interior elevators do not meet this requirement. You may want an attached or detached Accessory Dwelling Unit (ADU) on the property. This provides options for you or family members to have living space near the AFH. The more modifications you need to make, the longer it is before the business can bring in residents. This increases your initial start-up costs and delays the time frame in which the business becomes profitable.

Some people have raw land or a lot prepared for building as their starting point. They will need to put new construction on their property, which has both advantages and disadvantages. In new construction, you can design and build exactly what you want as a final structure. As designs and blueprints are carried out, building requirements can be met at every stage. You can be proactive about meeting codes and incorporating the latest technology. The downside is that new construction generally takes longer than conversions. There are carrying costs associated with delays, which could be due to permitting timelines, the banking process, or construction scheduling. As timelines for finishing construction get pushed out, leases and agreements will change and may not be finalized until everything is firmly in place.

Here is an estimate for the time needed for each part of the process. In general, the entire process of creating an AFH takes about a year. If you are starting with new construction, it often takes longer, and could be shorter if you are remodeling an existing house.

BUILDING AN AFH TIMELINE

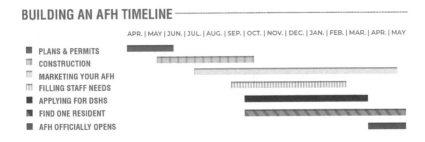

Next, consider the issue of location. There is good reason why the old real estate precept "location, location, location" has lasted through the years. Where your AFH is located makes a major difference in how attractive it will be to residents and their families. Analyze surrounding amenities such as shopping, eateries, public spaces and facilities, nearby medical care and hospitals, transportation options, travel times, neighborhood walkability, and places of worship. Take into consideration demographics of the surrounding area, population and construction growth patterns, property values and appreciation rates. This information will guide you in deciding if the area currently has attractive characteristics and will continue to offer them in the future.

If you have the potential of converting your current property into an Adult Family Home, all or most of these factors are already in place. Depending on where your property is located, there will be an established neighborhood with its unique characteristics. This is the existing social pattern in the area surrounding your planned AFH. Being able to connect with the neighborhood social pattern has been proven to support the quality of life and longevity among seniors.

This is where MyAFH can be of tremendous value, with its 20+ years of planning and executing conversions of existing single-family residential properties into Adult Family Homes in many different locations.

Location and ease of convertibility form the bottom line for an AFH business. These are multifaceted considerations that require expertise to evaluate thoroughly. It's best to get experienced advisors as early as possible to help you evaluate your property. An AFH management company can help you map out the neighborhood and larger community to understand its assets and limitations. It's like having a trusted guide to steer you through uncharted territory, rather than setting out on your own.

How To Evaluate Your Property for AFH Suitability

You may already own a house that you believe can be converted into an Adult Family Home, or there may be a house in your family that you are considering. One common scenario is exploring how suitable the home of elderly parents may be for modification into an AFH. If there is no potentially suitable house already in your family, you will be considering the purchase of a house or new construction for an AFH. In each of these scenarios, you will need to meet many of the same requirements for a suitable structure and landscape. Most existing houses can be converted into an AFH, and any residential area is acceptable as long as building and resident safety requirements can be met. Adult family homes must be single-family dwelling units, duplexes, or other type of dwelling for one or two families (per IRC#R101). Apartments and condominiums are not eligible.

It's advisable to start with a house that is a minimum of 2,000 square feet, since you will most likely need to add up to 1,000 more square feet to meet requirements. Ideally, the bottom floor should have room for six to eight individual bedrooms after additional square feet are built. In some cases, two residents may occupy one room, especially couples. There should be a room for caregivers to rest, preferably on the main resident floor. If the house has two stories, the top floor should be reserved for the Operator and caregiver housing. Although having resident rooms on the second floor is allowed, frail elderly or disabled residents should not have rooms on a second level, even with an elevator, due to fire safety requirements. It may be difficult or impossible for seniors to climb stairs. All stairs must have handrails for safety. If the house has a basement below the ground-level top floor, this could house Operators and caregivers. They prefer some separation in living spaces from the residents, although in some instances they share the same floor.

Perhaps the most important consideration is the elevation (egress) of the house. An ideal AFH house would be a rambler style where the first floor sits at ground level, situated on a flat lot. Steep lots are challenging for seniors to access safely, due to mobility and balance issues. When stairs are present, ramps for wheelchairs and walkers are necessary. A lot that is essentially level front to back is ideal. If there is uneven terrain or hills, these will need to be leveled for safety. Residents enjoy being able to walk and sit in nicely landscaped back yards, so even if there is a slight slope, a handrail should be installed to prevent falls. Another reason why ease of entry and exit is important relates to requirements for evacuation in the event of an emergency. Houses with difficult egress usually cannot formulate suitable evacuation plans.

There are numerous regulations for the house interior, which will be covered in detail in the following section. For an overview, think about the needs of elderly or disabled people as they navigate around bedrooms, bathrooms, and common areas such as dining and living rooms. Requirements stipulate that residents must be able to access toilets and bath/shower facilities easily. This means that doorways, hallways, and bathrooms must be wide enough for wheelchairs and for both the resident and a caregiver to comfortably maneuver around. Following American with Disabilities Act (ADA) building guidelines is important. As a minimum, there must be one toilet for every five people in the house. More toilets are preferred, and private baths will pay for themselves quickly with increased revenue. The house and grounds are required to be clean, hazard-free, and safe for residents.

Building Requirements for the Home

You must be able to verify these requirements when the initial house inspection takes place. These are not all the listed requirements (refer to your state's manual). Having a sound emergency plan with careful documentation and record-keeping is especially important since the country has contended with the COVID-19 pandemic. Awareness of this crisis and how many senior care facilities have been impacted is foremost in many people's minds. Having these plans and record systems can be a selling point for AFHs in attracting residents.

Listed below are the basic requirements, which will vary from state to state. In addition, there may be other requirements. Check with your state agencies.

- Single-family dwelling that meets current building code requirements.

- Is clean, sanitary, free of hazards, and safe for residents, both inside and outside.

- Has secure handrails at all stairs or steps inside and outside.

- Ramps with a specific state-mandated slope.

- Has approved fire extinguishers on each floor (2A:10B-C 5# rated).

- Has working smoke detectors on each floor, in hallways, in each resident bedroom, and in close proximity to the Operator/staff bedroom.

- Has windows that open easily, with intact screens on windows that can easily be removed in emergencies.

- Has first aid supplies with a first aid manual.

- Has emergency water and food supplies for a minimum of three days for six to ten people.

- Has a place to lock up medications, generally a closet or cabinet.

- Keeps cleaning supplies and other toxic substances out of reach of residents.

- Has adequate water supply and sewage; if the property has well water and private septic systems, these must be adequate in size and approved by DSHS.

- Formulates a written and workable disaster/emergency plan.

- Required electrical devices such as fire sprinklers when there are 8 residents, and generators for backup power if needed by specific circumstances.

- Uses record keeping processes that meet state requirements for adult family homes (in Washington WAC 388-76-10315 requirements).

If you choose to work with MyAFH, it is important to know that our standards exceed state regulations. Our belief is that residents of our homes deserve the best and safest environment possible, so additional building requirements will apply.

Bedroom Requirements

Since these rooms are the main dwelling space for residents, they have specific requirements for comfort and safety.

- There may be no more than two residents per room.

- A single room must have a minimum of 80 square feet of usable floor space, not including closet space and door swings.

- A double room must have a minimum of 120 square feet of usable floor space, not including closet space and door swings.

- Doors, including in the bedroom closet, must be openable from the inside and outside.

- There must be enough lighting in the room for residents to do what they want, and for staff to do what they need to do.

- There must be enough storage space in each bedroom to meet the needs of the residents.

Bathroom Requirements

A significant portion of home accidents happen in association with bathroom use. Particularly for elderly people, bathroom safety is a major requirement.

- Residents must be able to get to toilets and bath/shower facilities easily and safely.

- There must be one toilet for every five people in the house.

- The tub and shower must have grab bars and non-skid surfaces.

- Hot water temperature at fixtures accessible to residents must not exceed 120 degrees F.

Multiple AFH Properties

If you are considering operating more than one AFH, all the above requirements apply, plus several additional specifications. Each AFH unit or house must have separate staffing, separate living quarters, and separate addresses. There must be either a fire wall or a floor separating the two units, and they cannot have a common internal door. You will have double or multiples of the expenses and challenges of building and staffing, as well as ongoing maintenance and operations costs. You'll need to attract additional residents to fill your homes so the business can operate successfully. Of course, you'll receive the benefits of additional income when all your homes are filled and operating efficiently. There are other benefits of multiple homes, including being able to float caregiving staff among homes, sharing fixed costs, discounts on quantity purchases, and other benefits of scale.

Advantages of Using
an AFH Management Company

Management companies offer assistance with many aspects of the process and requirements of getting an AFH into operation. While there are several management companies offering services, MyAFH takes an especially compassionate approach due to our belief in personalized care for seniors and commitment to a more affordable option for senior living. Recognizing that this transitional period is fraught with difficulties, MyAFH extends caring and support to you and your loved ones along the way. The goal is to help make the transition smooth for everyone. Finding an optimal solution to senior housing and quality care starts with making informed decisions. MyAFH has the resources and experience to guide your decisions along the way to a better experience for your residents and your AFH business.

There are three ways that an AFH management company can provide assistance:

1. Manage aspects of your business for a fee while you remain the Owner.

2. Set up a long-term lease to operate your business with you as a landlord/Owner.

3. Form a partnership with you that shares the profits and losses of the business.

Some additional options include short-term relationships between you as Owner and an AFH management company. If you are already the Owner of an AFH, the management company can purchase your business and home when you are ready to sell or retire. This gets you out of the AFH business and is usually quite profitable since competitive prices are offered. It also provides a seamless transition for your residents. If you have an existing family home and want to convert it into an AFH, the management company can take over the process for you. Once the home is modified and licensed, residents recruited and staff hired, and ancillary services set up, the management company turns over a completely operational AFH to you. Or, you could pursue further relationships with the management company with various options.

> Management fees cover contractual agreements for services provided by an AFH management company. These services can include Management, Marketing, and Maintenance Packages. You have choices for what services are included in these packages.

Model #1: Management Fee

Investor Vignette: Harry* is a savvy investor who is a good money manager. He likes to be in control of the properties in which he invests and makes certain the Operators of his properties carry out their responsibilities competently. Harry bought a home and converted it into an AFH, having studied the advantages of this type of real estate investment. However, he is not interested in running the operations of the home himself. He wants to be able to pick and choose which services an AFH management company will carry out for him, so he decides to enter a contract for a management fee based upon their a la carte menu of services. He studies the choices, makes decisions, and agrees to services and fees.

Imagine yourself as Harry. The AFH management company enters a contract with you to operate certain aspects of the business for an agreed-upon monthly fee. You remain the Owner of the house and business. Management fees can fall into three different packages: management of the AFH operations, marketing the AFH business, and maintenance of the AFH property. With each package, there will be choices about what is included, and you can select which you want. The fees you pay depend upon which services you decide to contract with the AFH management company to provide. As property Owner, usually you must pay mortgages, building insurance, and property taxes. Additionally, you as Owner/landlord would collect rent from residents and pay all expenses.

The Management Package generally includes managing the care of residents and the operations of the AFH in providing this care. The AFH management company assures required licenses and certifications are attained and provides for staffing and training of caregivers and other personnel. This would include advertising staff positions, interviewing, hiring, organizing and evaluating staffing, and scheduling of caregivers and other personnel. In the package are administering human resources programs, maintaining required documents, and taking care of inventory needs. An important service is providing for a qualified, competent Resident Manager who oversees the care and operations requirements.

The Marketing Package commonly offered by the AFH management company assumes responsibility for attracting residents to their AFHs. Companies vary in how broadly their advertising ranges and how assertively they market their AFH clients. You should make certain that the marketing services are what you desire. Part of the services include advertising in media, a referral program, vacancy postings, lead management, and a call center for inquiries.

The Maintenance Package might vary a great deal, depending upon your budget and your ability to oversee all the different upkeep of house, property, yard and gardens, repairs, upgrades, and other improvements. Maintenance usually includes grounds and landscaping management, taking on repairs and renovations, and making sure the house and grounds continue to meet code and requirements. Online maintenance requests and mobile inspections assist in rapid and timely responses to maintenance needs.

In this model, you are hiring an AFH management company to assume the burden of day-to-day operations of this complex AFH business. As Owner/landlord, you could live on the property in an accessory dwelling unit (ADU) and interact with residents and staff. Your parents or other elderly family members could be among the residents. Without the multiple responsibilities of running the AFH, you'll have time for another job, hobbies, charity work, and travel. If the beds are full, you can attain a great cash flow. But, if the beds are not full, you may need to insert cash flow to keep the business running. It is incumbent on you to make sure your AFH management company is consistently fulfilling its obligations to keep the home a successful operation.

Example of Management Fees with MyAFH

The monthly fee for MyAFH is based on revenue. This fee will average between 5-15% of the gross monthly revenue of the particular adult family home. The reason for this fee range depends on how many services are selected for MyAFH to perform under the contract agreement. Standard practice is for this monthly fee to be paid regardless of how many beds are occupied. That said, it is possible to craft an agreement upon the fee to MyAFH being set on a fee-per-bed-filled basis. In this type of scenario it is to the advantage of MyAFH to ensure that the beds are occupied, and everyone benefits from a successful business.

Model #2: Lease Agreement

Investor Vignette: Yasmine* has years of experience in health care, both as a direct caregiver and manager of home care agencies and nursing home personnel. She became interested in another option for senior care that would be more personalized and inclusive of various levels of care. She explored the AFH business and decided this was the type of organization she was seeking. Yasmine was able to convert her elderly mother's home into an AFH, knowing that it would provide a perfect situation for her mom to age in place. After having devoted years to caregiving and supervision, Yasmine decided she was ready to delegate those responsibilities to others. So, she entered into a lease agreement with an AFH management company to operate her AFH.

Imagine yourself as Yasmine. As the Owner/landlord of the AFH, you enter into a long-term lease, usually 10 years, with the management company. You are leasing the business to the AFH management company, which is the tenant, which then takes over all responsibilities for operating the home. The tenant collects rents and pays expenses, in addition to carrying out all the marketing, maintenance, and management (staff-caregiving) packages described above. The Owner/landlord receives a guaranteed lease payment each month, regardless of the number of residents. As property Owner, you still must pay the home mortgage (if any), building insurance, and property taxes. The lease could be structured to stair-step as the number of residents increase, if needed.

In this model, you have even fewer responsibilities than in the Management Fee model. All of the advantages noted above apply. Some possible disadvantages include an unreliable management company that fails to operate a successful business. Depending upon how the lease is structured, you might lose money with unoccupied beds. If expenses outrun income, you'll need to insert money to bolster cash flow. If regulations are violated because the management company is lax, you could face costly fines or even be put out of business. Being an uninvolved Owner can lead to trouble. You would be well advised to keep close track of how the management company is running the AFH business, making sure it fulfills the agreements.

Example of Lease Agreement with MyAFH

One of the major advantages of the MyAFH Lease Agreement is that the first term is usually 10 years. This is favorable compared to typical residential leases of 1-2 years, which can result in vacancy gaps and tenant turnover that have negative impact on revenue stream and Net Operating Income.

The MyAFH Lease Agreement is stair-stepped according to what phase the project is in at any given time. During the first nine months, when the DSHS licensing is being obtained, lease payments to the real estate owner/landlord are set to cover the mortgage payment and allow for one senior resident to be cared for in the house. Although the lessee / business Owner/Operator will not hit profitability with only one resident, having that one resident jump-starts the process of getting inspections done and launching marketing and promotion of the home.

Upon obtaining DSHS licensing and occupancy permit, the monthly lease payment increases to the full agreed-upon amount. The Lease Agreement is the most popular option with current clients of MyAFH, in that it provides a guaranteed income stream with essentially no risk to the landlord.

There is room for negotiation in lease agreements, particularly when the AFH is located in a high-end neighborhood. Houses have higher values, taxes, and mortgages in such locations, and property owners might negotiate higher leases. If you own a million-dollar house in a desirable neighborhood, you may pay $4,000-5,000 per month in mortgage. In that instance, you could ask MyAFH to start lease payments the first year at $4,000 per month. Residents typically will pay more to live there, so when beds are filled, you could be earning around $45,000 in monthly income, and ask for a $6,000 monthly lease payment. It is expected that Owner/landlords will go into the red during the first year of startup, but they rapidly recap that through profits in subsequent years.

The Lease Agreement is the most popular option with clients of MyAFH. This arrangement provides guaranteed monthly lease payments with essentially no risk as long as the business prospers. This is a good option for those who want a sound income opportunity with very little risk. These figures will vary according to the particular AFH management company and the costs prevailing in the state or locale.[1]

Model #3: Partnership

Investor Vignette: Estella* has been running a successful AFH business for five years, and she enjoys the work, which gives her great fulfillment. Two years ago, she expanded and now owns two homes, which increased her workload and demanded more time away from her family. As her children launched into their careers and made plans to get married, Estella realized that she needed to lighten her workload to give more time to them. She did not want to completely relinquish running her two homes, however, since it meant so much to her. Estella examined options and chose to enter a partnership with an AFH management company. Under this arrangement, she would still be involved but would share responsibilities. The arrangements for various tasks could be negotiated and changed over time as needed.

Imagine yourself as Estella. Under the partnership model, all income and expenses are split between the Owner/landlord and the AFH management company. This is based on the profit/loss records after the net operating income (NOI) is determined. They share the benefits or detriments of how the business is operated, so both have a vested interest in seeing that the AFH business prospers. There is an "operator fee" that is paid to the AFH management company for operating the business, including all the aspects described above. This fee, usually in the range of 5-15% of gross revenues per month, is paid before profits are split each month.

If resident beds are filled or near capacity, this can be a very profitable option for both the Owner and the management company. Since both are working partners, they share responsibilities for overseeing how well the business is doing. Your level of involvement as Owner/landlord is variable depending upon personal interests. Someone who is the Owner of the real estate will have a different involvement than someone who is both the Owner and the Operator. Once again, you do not have to assume responsibility for the multiple aspects of running this complex business, since the management company provides marketing, maintenance, and management (staff-caregiving) packages. But you can be involved if you desire, and are encouraged to take part in caregiving as long as you have current credentials. Anyone involved in caregiving must acquire their certification and license from the state.

In this partnership model, you will share profits without assuming the major operational responsibilities, though your role is negotiable. You will share the cost if there is a need for cash infusion, but so will the management company. This shared scenario motivates the company to operate a well-managed business and avoid penalties and fines. Partnerships can be very lucrative for a home that is full, but will not make much money if all beds are not occupied. Through sharing the responsibilities for attracting residents, Owner/landlords and the management company both contribute toward business success.

*Each vignette is a real example. The actual names have been changed.

Example of Partnership with MyAFH

The Partnership Model is the second-most popular option for MyAFH clients at present. It is based upon shared responsibility, with both partners contributing to the success of the business in the various aspects of adult family home operation. There is risk-sharing because while both parties benefit from filled beds, they also share the potential from losses stemming from empty beds. So, everyone is motivated toward making the business a profitable success, as all are investing not just financially, but with time, energy, and expertise.

Monthly profits are calculated by taking the income based on the number of beds times the payment per bed (Gross Revenue) and subtracting all expenses for that particular home. Those monthly profits are then split between the partners at the agreed-upon contractual percentages.

This model offers the greatest flexibility for the Owner/Operator involved in the day-to-day running of an AFH business. He/she may be comfortable with a higher level of involvement in the beginning, but have the desire to scale back their commitment over time as conditions in their life change. For that reason this model has a unique appeal.

Keep in mind that when you enter into this type of partnership agreement, you always retain the choice to exit the business and sell your AFH to MyAFH at an agreed-upon price. With MyAFH having the first right of refusal, you are assured of their offering a competitive sales price, and of a smooth transition for your residents because of their involvement in your operations.

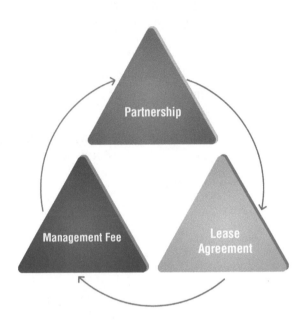

3 RELATIONSHIPS WITH AN AFH MANAGEMENT COMPANY

Consider Your Options and Move Forward

This chapter has helped you examine whether your property is right for an AFH, and what options you may have for acquiring or remodeling a suitable property. You have looked at costs and timelines, licensing and building requirements, and the levels of involvement you can choose if you select to work with an AFH management company. Examples of financial scenarios have been provided to assist you in seeing how these might fit with your situation.

Consider the advantages and disadvantages of these three relationships carefully. AFH management companies such as MyAFH are designed to assist you with your senior living facility business. This includes giving you an in-depth understanding about the process and tasks that must be accomplished. Their extensive knowledge of AFH licensing and policies, as well as optimal management strategies and safety requirements, will help you run a successful business.

You will come to appreciate the benefits of teaming up with an AFH management company even more once you have digested the details of operating a senior living facility, discussed in the next chapter. Now, you are prepared to move forward in this process. The next chapter unravels the specifics and illuminates details of operating an Adult Family Home.

6

OPERATING
A SENIOR LIVING FACILITY

VENTURING INTO THE ARENA of operating a senior living facility is a significant undertaking. To arrive at this decision point, you have traveled
through several stages of exploration and assessment of your goals
and capabilities. First, you learned about the senior care and housing
industry, designing your map through this territory and gaining a
solid understanding of the various types of living facility options.
You've weighed the pros and cons and decided which works best
for you and your family's situation. Having settled on an Adult Family
Home as your preferred option, you then determined what level of
involvement you want as an investor and how much you want to
participate in its operation. You looked at whether you have what it
takes to "go it alone" or whether partnering with an AFH management
company is the best approach for you in developing an AFH business.

The crucial consideration of whether your property is right for an
AFH was the next step. This took you through evaluating your family
home to see if it could be converted into an AFH. You might have

explored other options, such as buying a suitable house or launching a new construction. During these considerations, you reviewed the state requirements for both property conversion and care of residents, learning that this is a highly regulated business that needs careful and continuing attention to all the details of compliance. In this process, you weighed the merits of differing relationships with an AFH management company, such as leasing your property to them, utilizing various aspects of their services, or forming a partnership to operate your AFH business together.

Steps to Your AFH Decision

At this point, you have:

- Learned about senior living options.
- Examined which type of senior living and care is best for you and your family.
- Developed a map for your approach to decision-making.
- Considered why and how you will invest in the AFH business.
- Weighed the level of involvement you want in AFH operations.
- Evaluated your property for conversion into an AFH.
- Decided whether or not to use an AFH management company.

Now, as you move forward in this process, you'll need to delve into the details of what every AFH owner needs to know—especially if you're planning to go it alone. This chapter will cover key points in operating an Adult Family Home. Each point provides essential information for running a successful AFH business and meeting the numerous state regulations; for example, there are over 700 rules in Washington State. These points include caregiver qualifications with training and certification requirements, owner and operator qualifications and what is required as an AFH business owner, referral agents (what they are and how they help), and the importance of landscaping, supplies, maintenance, and legal advice. The role of technology will be examined along with current trends, and the critical roles of oversight and safety will be described for both the property and residents.

After going over the many details of these points, the chapter will discuss the benefits of using an AFH management company. You may still decide that you can handle running an AFH business on your own. However, it will be instructive to know what assistance you can receive from teaming up with an experienced management company.

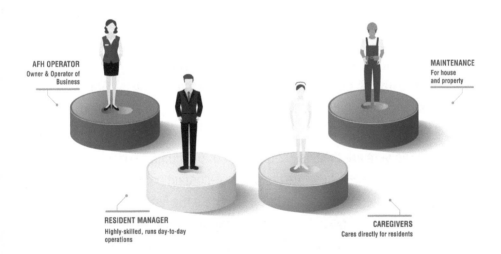

AFH OPERATOR
Owner & Operator of Business

MAINTENANCE
For house and property

RESIDENT MANAGER
Highly-skilled, runs day-to-day operations

CAREGIVERS
Cares directly for residents

Like all healthcare entities, quality difference results in outcome difference. However, unlike hospitals and clinics, most elder care facilities do not have significant oversight or checks and balances. Additionally, staff training can be variable, worse with the high rates of turnover within the industry. As this is care for our most vulnerable population, consistency, thorough training, comprehensive yet practical protocols, and unwavering oversight result in a safer environment for staff and patients alike.

Caregiver Qualifications

In the process of setting up an AFH, obtaining the proper training requirements will be one of the first steps. This step takes place early and should happen in conjunction with acquiring a suitable physical location for the property you are planning to turn into an AFH. For an efficient approach, you shouldn't work for months obtaining licensing for staff *then* start looking for the right location. Likewise, there is little point in finding and then purchasing or leasing a business location, only to have it sit empty for months while you finish licensing requirements. This delays the process of opening the business. For a successful AFH, you must simultaneously work to obtain the proper training needed along with the correct facility to operate the business. Doing all these things simultaneously requires a lot of time and expertise, even with help.

Caregivers are the basic foundation of providing services to residents of an AFH. These are the point-of-contact people with whom residents interact on a daily basis. They are the face of your AFH to the families who place their seniors in your care. Thus, it's critically important that you have well-trained caregivers who are also caring, compassionate people. There are two types of caregivers, the Home Care Aide (HCA) and the Certified Nursing Assistant (CNA). Both classifications have similar training requirements, although those for the CNA are a little more extensive. Both must complete 75 hours of training before they are eligible to work in an AFH. About 80%

of this education can be accomplished online. A few classes must be done in person, so it's important to plan time wisely in order to meet credentialing timelines.

Caregivers, whether Home Care Aides or Certified Nursing Assistants, must apply for the Nursing Assistant Registration (NAR) with the state. Once that application is received, the countdown to becoming registered begins. In Washington State, the caregiver applicant has 200 days to take and pass the state exam in order to receive their credential. They will have two chances to pass this exam during those 200 days. If they fail to finish the process within this time, they can no longer be employed at a licensed AFH facility. Although it's possible to work privately, such as being directly hired by a family without going through an agency, the family has no liability protection with a non-credentialed caregiver unless they purchased it on their own.

The 75-hour training/certification course[1] includes:

38 HOURS
Core Basic Training

5 HOURS
Orientation & Safety

8 HOURS
Mental Health Training

8 HOURS
Dementia Specialty Training

16 HOURS
Hands-on Skill Training

Additional requirements for an AFH may include:
• Nurse core delegation
• Nurse diabetes delegation
• CPR/first aid card
• WA state food handlers card (1 hour)

HCA and CNA Certification

As you read these training stipulations for staff, keep in mind that training required by MyAFH exceeds the minimums set by the state. This is not true for every AFH management company.

HCA (Home Care Aide) Certification

The HCA certification course meets the minimum requirements to operate an adult family home. This training focuses on the actual care needed in an AFH. HCA training consists of the areas included in the 75-hour course and can be taken at a variety of times based on personal schedules (weekends only, weekdays, weekday evenings). The length of time needed to complete the training depends on which schedule is selected.

CNA (Certified Nursing Assistant) Certification

The CNA program is a little more thorough and includes tasks that are performed in a hospital setting. This training is relevant to the work performed in an AFH but is not tailored to just this setting. CNA is a good basic certification to have, but does not necessarily include some aspects specific to working in an AFH (Orientation and Safety course, Dementia Specialty course, and Mental Health Specialty course). Many AFH operators prefer the HCA certification because of its specific focus.

Orientation and Safety Course

This course addresses the basics of working in long-term care and must be taken prior to beginning as a caregiver, unless exempt from training. It covers requirements that a prospective AFH caregiver must meet in order to provide services to residents in a licensed AFH setting. Also included is the process each prospective AFH operator needs to follow before applying for their AFH license. Orientation takes two hours, and safety training takes three hours. The course must be approved by the state.

Long-Term Care Worker Basic Training

In this course, the caregivers and operators study multiple aspects of the elder care industry and providing care to seniors in long-term facilities, including AFHs. They learn basic skills and information needed to provide hands-on personal care. In addition, they study topics unique to the care needs of elderly and developmentally disabled populations. Coursework may include training in mental health and dementia. Operators must complete the course prior to licensure of the home (unless exempt from training); caregivers must complete it within 120 days of hire (unless exempt). The state must approve the curriculum to fulfill licensing and credentialing requirements.

Dementia Specialty Training

This course includes the knowledge, skills, and competencies for understanding behaviors, emotions, and actions of those suffering with dementia. Dementia is one of the leading conditions of residents entering care in AFHs at this time. As seniors age, the risk of developing dementia increases significantly, and most will have some difficulty with mental functioning during their lifetimes. Because of this, the course is highly recommended and extracurricular study of this topic is advised. The course must be approved by the state.

Mental Health Specialty Training

This course includes the knowledge, skills, and competencies for understanding various mental health problems. It's very important for AFH caregivers to be capable of handling the behaviors, emotions, and actions of vulnerable adults with mental health diagnoses, and know-how to properly care for them. Working with patients with behavioral, cognitive, or psychiatric illnesses can be very challenging. The same is true of complex and infectious disease processes. Appropriate training is a necessity for both patient and staff safety. The course must be approved by the State.

Nurse Delegation Course

The nurse delegation course trains AFH caregivers in specific tasks that are normally performed only by licensed nurses. These tasks include the administration of prescription medications, blood glucose testing, and others. A licensed nurse delegates (trains) the AFH caregivers to carry out these tasks for residents of the facility. The AFH caregiver being trained must be a Nursing Assistant (registered or certified) or a Home Care Aide (certified) and complete the Nurse Delegation core training before accepting a delegated task. Included in the course are specifications of how the delegations are to be performed and the importance of always having proper training of caregivers for the safety of the residents.

Special Focus on Diabetes Course

The nurse delegation special focus on diabetes course is mandatory for any AFH caregivers and operators who will care for residents with diabetes. This course details the basics of administering insulin and other medical needs for a resident with diabetes. The above requirements for Nursing Assistants and Home Care Aides apply.

Developmental Disabilities Course

The developmental disabilities course is mandatory for any AFH caregivers and operators in a home with residents having any type of developmental disability (DD). Some forms of DD are intellectual disabilities, Down syndrome, autism, Tourette syndrome, cerebral palsy, spina bifida, and Fragile X syndrome. Many times developmental disability residents are younger in age. Some AFHs have been specifically designed to house only DD residents. The course must be approved by the state, the AFH workers must take and pass a test, and the course must be completed within 120 days of hiring.

HIV Training

The HIV Training course is mandatory for all AFH operators. This course gives a thorough explanation and offers a good understanding of the basics of what HIV is, how it is transmitted, safety precautions the AFH staff must be aware of, and how to take action in case of exposure.

CPR and First Aid Certification

This is another mandatory course for the operator and also for all caregiving staff. This course teaches the basic functions of giving CPR as well as the skills for any First Aid to be given in the home. It must be completed within 30 days of employment if directly supervised by someone with a valid card. If not, it must be completed before starting to provide care.

Tuberculosis Testing

A tuberculosis skin test (PPD) is given within three days of being hired to work in an AFH. If the test is negative, a second PPD is administered one to three weeks later. If the test is positive, a chest X-ray is done to verify there is no active TB. A more accurate blood test called Quantiferon Gold can also be done and is acceptable to rule out active TB.

Operator Qualifications

There are multiple steps to becoming an operator. Many people hear that AFHs have great cash flow and decide they want to open one. However, you must have at least the basics of a medical background to become a licensed operator. This includes a minimum of 1,000 hours (roughly 6 months) experience of hands-on care to seniors or vulnerable adults, as well as completing specified courses. It is an arduous process. Even if the operator (business owner) does not plan to be doing any direct care, the 75-hour course must be completed along with application for the NAR (Nursing Assistant Registration). The purpose is to ensure that operators can become involved in care if necessary, and properly supervise their staff.

The AFH operator must complete several courses in order to be eligible to open and operate an Adult Family Home. Operators must receive their license before starting to operate the home. If the resident manager of the AFH is someone other than the operator, the same courses also apply. Much of the 75 hours of training is the same as that for caregivers, but there are some additional stipulations for operators and resident managers. Before providing care to residents in the AFH, operators and resident managers must complete (unless exempt):

- First Aid and CPR

- Orientation (2 hours)

- Safety Training (3 hours)
- 70-Hour Long-Term Care Worker Basic Training

Adult Family Home Orientation

The AFH Orientation is a mandatory 8-hour course for anyone in order to become an AFH operator, but it might be beneficial if you are even *considering* becoming a operator. This is actually a "crash course" of all the items that are needed to operate an AFH, and explains many basics of how to run a successful AFH business. Many people take this class before and even after taking any of the other mandatory courses. The class must be completed within one year of submitting an application to open an AFH. It is taught by state health department staff. (This class is not required for resident managers.)

AFH Administrator Training

The AFH administrator training is a minimum of 56 hours of training on topics related to the licensing and operation of an AFH. All applicants who submit an application for an AFH license (approximate cost $2,750), and an operator planning to open a second AFH, must complete this training. The course is usually offered during evenings or weekends at local colleges or universities that have been certified as training locations by the state. Not only is this course mandatory, it also will help shed light on exactly what it will be like to own and operate an AFH as an operator. Be very thorough in your note-taking and seek a sound understanding of what you will be getting into.

1,000 Documented Hours Working Directly with Seniors or Vulnerable Adults

The most time-consuming part of becoming a licensed AFH operator is the required 1,000 hours of direct care to vulnerable adults.

This generally is an issue for someone who has just started the process to become an operator and has no medical background. Operators currently licensed as an RN, CNA, HCA, or LPN usually have no issues with this requirement as they already have fulfilled the needed hours. This rule has a solid foundation, since you should not attempt to enter this business without any medical knowledge or exposure to health care.

Food Handling and Safety

The Food Worker Card is mandatory for anyone in the AFH who will be handling food for the residents at any time. This includes the operator, caregivers, and volunteer help. The course deals with the dangers of improperly cooked food and proper handling of all food in the home. Operators or employees with food handler permits prior to June 30, 2005, must take 0.5 hours of continuing education per year to maintain the card. A food handler permit is not required for long-term care workers who began working after June 30, 2005; provided they completed basic training and were trained on safe food handling practices. Documentation of this must be kept on file by the operator.

Continuing Education

Both operators and caregivers are required to complete 12 hours per year of continuing education to remain current in the care of seniors and vulnerable persons. Courses acceptable to fulfill this requirement are specified by the state and are generally available through colleges and universities or on-line.

Training Requirement Summary for Adult Family Homes

TYPE OF TRAINING	AFH PROVIDER OR RESIDENT MANAGER	AFH CAREGIVER (LONG-TERM CARE WORKER)	DSHS (STATE) APPROVAL OF COURSE
First-aid and CPR	Before providing care to the clients	Within 30 days of employment or prior	✗
Orientation (2 hrs)	Before providing care to the clients	Before providing care to the clients	✓
Safety Training (3 hrs)	Before providing care to the clients	Before providing care to the clients	✓
Orientation to the facility	N/A	Each AFH must ensure onsite staff orientation	✗
70-hr LTC Worker Basic Training	Before licensure of the home	Within 120 days of hire	✓
Specialty Training (DD, Dementia, MH)	Prior to or within 120 days of providing care	Prior to or within 120 days of providing care	✓
Nurse Delegation Core/Diabetes	NA/HCA Certified, complete before task	NA/HCA Certified, complete before task	✓ (state instructors)
Continuing Education	12 hours/year	12 hours/year	✓
Food Handling & Safety	Prior to providing care, 0.5 hours CE	Prior to providing care	✓
AFH Administrator Training	Before submitting app. for AFH license	N/A	✓ (community colleges/universities)
AFH Orientation Class	Within 1 year of AFH application	N/A	✓ (state instructors)

*Based on Washington State Department of Social and Health Services Aging and Long-Term Support Administration (ALTSA); https://www.dshs.wa.gov/altsa/training/training-reuirements-adult-family-homes[31]

Referral Agencies and Agents

The senior care industry has so many facets to navigate that it is helpful for families to seek expert advisors, called referral agents, when searching for a suitable AFH. These referral agents are a subset of the industry and offer varying levels of experience, information, involvement, and guidance. Some work for nonprofit senior organizations or state agencies, while others are independent businesses. They will have differing connections and relationships with long-term care facilities and their owners.

The State of Washington laws describe a senior care referral agency in WAC 388-76, RCW (Revised Code of Washington, Elder and Vulnerable Adult Referral Agency Act) Title 18, Chapter

Referral agents are paid by commission. Usually, their fees are paid by Adult Family Homes or other senior care facilities for referring clients. Thus, the family seeking an AFH is not charged a fee. While this service may be "free" to the family, it does have associated fees paid by facilities that get referrals.

18.330: "Placement agency" is an "elder or vulnerable adult referral agency" as defined in chapter 18.330.010 RCW and means a "business or person who receives a fee from or on behalf of a vulnerable adult seeking a referral to care services or supportive housing or who receives a fee from a care services provider or supportive housing provider because of any referral provided to or on behalf of a vulnerable adult."[3]

Referral agencies are not licensed by the state but there are different entities that will "certify" a person after completing a training course. In general, they aim to simplify the senior care process by assisting those searching for senior care to get connected with providers of care directly. Many agents have lists of Adult Family Homes and other types of assisted living facilities, with descriptions of the range of services provided, locations, costs, and availability. These agents talk with seniors and their families to determine preferences and goals in seeking assisted living care. Many have websites and search tools that allow families to search for care in a chosen area and filter down results based on specific care needs such as dementia, mental health, and developmental disabilities. Larger agencies such as DSHS Locator and Adult Family Home Council may have hundreds of possible placements to select among.

Smaller referral agencies tend to have a personal touch that can be helpful, but they may be limited in how much information they have about various types of facilities. The large groups have complex systems in place to keep track of information gathered and status of facilities they work with. Still, there is no guarantee they have personal knowledge of the area, facility, or people involved. One benefit of referral agents is that they will have screened facilities on their list to ensure these are properly licensed and have qualified care providers. Most agents will meet with families

Different areas of medicine work smoothly together when there are personal relationships between staff, enhancing trust. This is also true of the relationship between the AFH operators and the many entities involved in the care of their residents: primary care, insurance, visiting providers, transportation services etc. Cultivated relationships are an advantage to everyone, including the residents.
—Dr. Morris

and seniors, answer questions, discuss options, and set up visits to facilities. They can provide a list of questions to ask when talking to a prospective facility, as well as things to watch for during the tour of the home.

When working on their own to find a placement, most people will be overwhelmed with the choices available. They may make choices because the facility is close by or familiar, only to later discover that it does not meet their needs. Since finding the right placement is so important, referral agents have become a popular service business in recent years. When selecting a referral agent, it's important to make sure they are following the laws set out by the Elder and Vulnerable Adult Placement Referral Agency Act (RCW 18.330). The law requires that you read and sign a Disclosure of Services statement that includes agency and client information, details regarding the fee to be received (and refund policy) for the referral, description of services provided, and frequency of facility tours by the agency. Included should be contact information for the Office of the Attorney General if a complaint needs to be filed.

Referral agents should use a standardized intake form for clients, adhering to healthcare confidentiality laws (HIPAA). Included are medical history, diagnoses, medications, and health concerns. You will be asked why you are seeking services, current living situation, if assistance is needed with activities of daily living, and any behavioral concerns, dementia, or developmental disabilities. Basic understanding of current financial situation, preferences on location, and other things important to your specific situation are included. Most agencies operate on a private pay basis with the senior and their family. Although their help is free to the family, agencies have contracts with facilities that pay fees if sent clients. If the client is on Medicaid or Medicare, the referral agency cannot collect a referral fee for services covered by Federal or State health care programs.

Within 30 days of making a referral, the agent must inform you if any referred facilities are in violation of legal codes. Agencies must keep records of referrals made for at least six months, maintain $1 million general and professional liability insurance, and perform criminal background checks every two years on owners, operators, and employees who have contact with vulnerable adults.

Advantages of referral agents for the operators of senior care include management and wide exposure of their AFH listing, direct connection with potential residents and families, scheduling tours of the facility, staff support, range of solutions for individual AFH needs or issues, and networking opportunities within the industry.

SUMMARY PROS & CONS OF USING REFERRAL AGENTS

PROS	CONS
Agent saves time and simplifies process of evaluating wide range of facilities	Information agent has could be limited to only select facilities
Agent has information based on location, care needed, and price range	Agent fee is based on final price family agrees to pay the facility; determine who pays fee (family or provider); could be expensive
Agents help families narrow choices and ask the right questions when talking to prospective facilities	Family using multiple agents can be confused about information source and application; might use disreputable agent unless checking

Landscaping

The construction of structures on the Adult Family Home property, changes to the existing terrain, and the addition of plants are all part of landscaping. Taking into consideration the footprint of AFH structures, landscaping includes the planning, laying out, and construction of gardens that create usable space for outdoor activities around the house. These are intended to enhance the appearance of the home and improve the quality of life for residents. Outdoor living areas are attractive and augment aesthetic appeal when potential residents are touring the facilities. They offer a pleasant, peaceful space for residents to enjoy during their time at the home.

Supplies

The initial inventory of supplies for new homes includes everything such as appliances, furniture, first aid, and even utensils. Once the home is fully stocked, a weekly inventory report is made that helps with keeping supplies up to date and available. Supplies include resident care items, cleaning products, incontinence supplies, food, household items, nutritional supplements, and linens. Since the onset of COVID-19, additional supplies for personal protective equipment (PPE) and test kits are necessary.

Maintenance

Comprehensive maintenance plans are essential to keeping the AFH running at peak efficiency. These are required to remain in compliance with governmental rules and guidelines. Routine maintenance inspections are conducted quarterly, and other inspections and maintenance items are available when requested. Good maintenance programs are designed to keep the building and property in top condition and avoid unnecessary repairs. When repairs or changes are needed, effective property maintenance will ensure that customers get the best pricing available.

Legal and Regulations Compliance

There is a saying in clinical medicine: "if it's not documented it didn't happen." Transfer of clinical information, verbally or with documentation, is one of the areas of medicine known to have a high rate of medical errors. Good documentation is a hallmark of quality and a necessity for good care. Trusting such a critically important aspect of senior care to a substandard facility is not what most people want for their loved ones.
—Dr. Morris

Among the most challenging aspects of operating an AFH is making certain that you comply with rules and regulations. The majority of these are set by the state. Obtaining sound legal advice and accurately drawn contracts are also vitally important to avoid costly legal battles. Although there are hundreds of regulations to meet, the greatest numbers of violations involve only a few of these. The top violations and legal mistakes of AFH operators are covered below.

1. Documentation inadequacies constitute the number one citation against AFH operators.[4] At the top of the documentation list is failure to properly document medications. Medication administration and recording can be the most complicated part of caring for the elderly. There are different systems that AFHs can use to keep medications organized and administered properly, but the primary cause of mistakes is human error. AFH staff must adhere to the "6 rights" of medication administration:

> #1 Right Client
> #2 Right Medication
> #3 Right Time
> #4 Right Dose
> #5 Right Route
> #6 Right Documentation

A misstep in any of these can result in a citation. Other common inadequacies cited include negotiated care plans, resident charts, logs, and forms. All these must be meticulously kept to be in compliance with state regulations.

2. Contracts that are not well written can be another pitfall. Best practice includes using an attorney who is familiar with AFH requirements. Attempting to draw up your own contract without legal counsel is not in your best interest. An incomplete or poorly written contract is a significant risk and will eventually get you into trouble.

3. Safety and maintenance are in the top three sources for citations. There are numerous requirements to provide a safe environment for residents, both inside and outside the home. Failure to keep the property maintained adds to safety issues, and will catch

the eye of the regular unscheduled state inspections. The AFH operator is best advised to keep on top of these factors and avoid costly citations that can easily reach into the $1000s.

4. Residents rights violations and policies related to abuse can be a source of trouble for AFH operators. Background checks on staff and required training help avoid such issues as physical and emotional abuse on site. Financial abuse is a sensitive but fairly common rights violation, usually committed by family members. They may ask the senior for money, or if they have power of attorney, they may spend the senior's money inappropriately. It is legal for an AFH operator to request a financial statement from the family before a resident moves in, but not after. It becomes tricky when the family does not provide accurate financial information.

5. Challenging behaviors by a resident can create legal problems for AFH operators. At times the family will not provide accurate information about the resident's actual care needs, and the truth comes out once in the facility. You may contend that the AFH is unable to meet these care needs, and thus the resident should be moved to another facility. But, proving this can be tricky and might lead to litigation.

6. Doing your due diligence when acquiring an AFH property or existing business is important in order to avoid costly legal battles. You need to research the property history with the state, federal, and city regulatory agencies and make sure there are no outstanding legal issues, late payments, or investigations in effect. These types of problems will limit your ability to operate the AFH effectively and add to costs.

Safety

There are numerous state regulations to protect the physical safety of residents in an AFH. It is mandatory that the AFH operator ensure these are met and undergo regular reevaluation of property, house, staff, and operations. Any deficiencies must be corrected quickly, or citations are sure to follow. Another aspect of safety involves how to reassure families that their loved one will be safe within the house. This is a wider-ranging issue and involves the working atmosphere within each home, including operators, caregivers, and other staff.

The operator must have familiarity with each resident in order to speak knowledgeably and answer questions accurately when speaking with health care professionals, families, state investigators, and others. They should ask the family about additional safety features needed by the resident, such as medic alerts, motion sensors, exit monitoring, or other technologies for the resident's room. As a long-term safety enhancement, building trust with the AFH care team will grow their strengths and invest in the next generation of managers, caregivers, and operators.

> The warm, personalized relationships AFH operators and caregivers have with residents is beneficial to everyone involved. For operators and caregivers this is part of their labor of love: they are in health care to help people, not just earn a living. Residents fare better in a home-like environment, the basic premise of the AFH model versus the corporate one. Families find reassurance when their loved ones are with familiar caring people.
> —Dr. Morris

The caregivers participate in an intimate setting where the group, both staff and residents, look after one another and become a family of its own. A consistent care team builds relationships and familiarity, so when subtle changes happen, they are noticed and reported to the right people in a timely manner. A cohesive staff and resident group enhances the ability to meet needs as they change and obtain appropriate support from the proper level in the organization. As an example, COVID-19 precautions were easier to implement in a short time period within AFHs as compared to Assisted Living Facilities (ALFs). This was due to the smaller, more familiar and cohesive groups in AFHs.

Well-run AFHs also offer a measure of safety to the families of their residents. Families can feel reassured that trained professionals will handle challenging behaviors such as sundowning, wandering, exit seeking, and aggression. These professionals have the ability to redirect, protect, and engage the resident in healthy ways that promote safety. When this burden of care is transferred from the family to a trained professional team, family members can return to normal activities and relationships. There is peace of mind for the family in knowing the staff has the same goals in caring for their loved one with compassion, respect, and dignity. This can ameliorate family fears about the wellbeing and safety of their senior.

> Working with residents who have dementia or delirium can be exhausting. In the absence of experienced, knowledgeable and professional staff, the situation may become non-therapeutic or unsafe. It is often these behaviors that make living at home untenable, requiring placement in a facility like an AFH. Training, protocols, medical oversight, and a tailored built environment are critical for comfort and safety.
> —Dr. Morris

Oversight

The issue of who is accountable for oversight is important in the senior care industry. Ensuring compliance with regulations is one aspect of responsible oversight best undertaken by the operator of the AFH. The state does make inspections, often unannounced, and will assess fines for compliance failures. Many safety problems may be identified, both within the home and in the access and grounds.

Constant vigilance is necessary to make sure residents remain safe in their rooms and the facility, everything from proper medication administration to keeping hot water at the required temperature. It is far better for the manager or operator to find infractions than for the state to discover them. Using an AFH management company adds an additional layer of oversight and accountability.

Perhaps the least reported safety violations are around miscommunication with residents and abuse by staff or family. These issues are not readily apparent on a state inspection visit, especially with residents having decreased mental function. Oversight can be provided by an alert and observant operator, who can intervene early before the problems get out of hand. Having an AFH management company increases vigilance and offers a source for mediation, thus enhancing safety on both sides: family can seek support dealing with caregivers, and caregivers can get help handling difficult or abusive family members. Without such an intermediary, the only recourse can be state authorities within agencies for elder abuse and senior living facility safety. Pursuing such issues through the state bureaucracy can be challenging and slow.

When you team up with an AFH management company, oversight for your AFH is increased, and additional resources available for handling problems. A "lone wolf" AFH operator might not observe details of compliance, safety, or abuse problems. Or, there may be a tendency to overlook some details since dealing with them can be overwhelming.

Technology

Adult Family Homes have a unique need for new medical and healthcare delivery technology. AFHs also receive a special benefit from these technological advances. The most clear-cut technological advancement that benefits elderly patients, including those in AFHs, is telehealth. This is quickly becoming the standard of care for many healthcare encounters. Advantages for AFH residents are overwhelming. Avoiding the inconvenience and medical risk of office visits far outweighs any benefit from in-person physical exams. Telehealth evaluation is augmented by the skills of AFH staff who see residents regularly and have some medical training. Residents are safer at home as they avoid exposure to infections and are kept healthy through strict protocols and medical oversight at the AFH.

Envision this situation where a resident must travel to the doctor's office or clinic for evaluation. Getting to a clinic visit is often an ordeal for elderly patients. They must be taken from the home, put into the vehicle, spend time in the car, get from the vehicle to the clinic (often by wheelchair, taking an elevator), stay in the waiting room, move into the exam room, and then do the whole process in reverse. Frequently, patients report being exhausted by the activity. In addition, many elderly patients suffer adverse events due to stress when visiting clinics: anxiety, exhaustion, discomfort, fainting, or other adverse event. This can result in sudden transfer to the emergency department for evaluation. It is easy to imagine the stress this puts on elders with dementia, physical disabilities, or who are frail and prone to falls. This is even more risky when some of these visits occur because the patient is sick! Much of this can be avoided using telehealth technology.

Urgent medical oversight using telehealth will ameliorate one of the main reasons for over and underuse of the emergency room for the elderly. Often a phone conversation with a consulting nurse is not enough to decide when the risks of taking a patient to the emergency room outweigh the benefits. A telehealth visit with a medical provider (MD, DO, ARNP, PA) where they can see and talk to the patient and the caregiver, review notes and take vital signs can be the difference between life and health. Hospitals are not benign places for the elderly; they are a source of infection and significant risk of harm to these patients. While hospitals are also a place of comfort and healing, hospital visits only outweigh the risks when the patient is truly ill, and the illness is amenable to treatment there.

Benefits of Telehealth for Seniors in AFHs:

- Day-to-day caregivers present
- Doctor sees and speaks with patient virtually
- Conference can include family
- Decreased stress for patient
- Avoid inconvenience and discomfort
- Avoid dangers (falls, fainting risks)
- Avoid exposure to infections
- Reduce risks of worsening dementia and disorientation

Use of artificial intelligence (AI) is going to revolutionize the daily health care of residents. AI will enhance everything from voice-activated calling "I need help" to scheduling medications reliably, entertainment, and improving wellbeing. Although no one knows exactly how this new technology is going to affect all parts of life, it seems the benefits will be substantial. Using AI technology to avoid human errors lends an added layer of medical security.

Even though the training of MyAFH's staff is robust, and this should apply to all AFHs with better national standards, the additional ability of AI to detect problems and make corrections will benefit safety goals.

Use of telehealth can prevent tragic outcomes and extremely costly care. Here are examples of how the triage process of evaluating a possible illness and deciding on a course of care can be vastly improved with this technology.

☒

TRIAGE WITHOUT TELEHEALTH

A 90-year-old AFH resident develops a cough, but no signs of serious illness such as fever and increased respiratory rate. Using telehealth, the patient receives a full evaluation from a doctor that includes past medical history, showing the patient is very healthy despite his age.

Due to delays, the patient arrives at the hospital after midnight, appearing delirious due to disruption of routine and lack of sleep. Even though there are no signs of pneumonia, the ER staff admits the patient because of delirium, considering it unsafe to return him to the AFH

Continued over-stimulation by bright lights and commotion in the hospital cause the patient to aspirate food, which quickly leads to aspiration pneumonia. As the patient gets sicker, requiring ventilation and IVs, the family withdraws care, and the elderly patient is allowed to die in the hospital.

The 90-year-old patient had requested to die at home (in the AFH), but instead died uncomfortably at the hospital. After the funeral, the family learns they are responsible for tens of thousands of dollars in medical and hospital bills.

☑

TRIAGE WITH TELEHEALTH

A 90-year-old AFH resident develops a cough, but no signs of serious illness such as fever and increased respiratory rate. When the AFH worker calls a triage nurse with limited information, the nurse is concerned about pneumonia and sends an ambulance.

Via video, the doctor hears the patient state he feels well despite the new cough. Vital signs are normal, no different than the past seven days, and several AFH staff on-site report the patient looks well to them.

The family is brought into the teleconference, and the doctor learns that the patient does not want to be transported to the hospital unless absolutely necessary. He had developed delirium in prior hospital visits, and wishes to die peacefully at home (AFH).

Review of medications shows that he was recently started on Lisinopril, an anti-hypertension drug notorious for causing a dry cough. The doctor recommends stopping the Lisinopril, and within days, the cough resolves.

The telehealth visit took 15 minutes and resolved the 90-year-old patient's situation without his leaving the AFH. His wishes were honored, and his family satisfied. The bill to the family was a $50 co-pay.

How technology will continue to change medicine is unclear, though there will certainly be some growing pains as the change progresses. It is clear, though, that for elderly patients, there is great benefit to be had using technology. The format of the AFH is well-suited to adopting and benefiting from these advancements in the way we practice medicine.

Benefits of an AFH Management Company

Operating a senior living facility, in particular, an Adult Family Home, calls for a wide range of skills and a commitment to high standards of elder care. The requirements are numerous and demand capacity for attention to details and thoughtful planning. While there are many sources of information and assistance in this complex business, you would do well to consider an AFH management company as a partner in your AFH. These management companies will differ in their approach and capacities, but in general, should provide within their organizational structure the expertise to guide you in each step of the process.

MyAFH, family-owned and operated since 1995, is specifically designed to assist clients with all aspects of their AFH business. The founders saw a need within the senior care industry to bring together a team of qualified experts who can assist AFH operators by removing the burdens of finances, compliance, and operations in the business. Their services provide an in-depth understanding of the process and tasks that need to be accomplished. The company has extensive experience in AFH licensing and policies, including management and safety, originally in Washington State and now in several other states.

The professional team at MyAFH specializes only in Adult Family Homes. They can help you locate, open, and manage your AFH successfully. The team believes that finding and providing quality senior care starts with making an informed decision. With their resources and experience, they will support you every step along the way to a better experience for your family, your residence, and your business.

MyAFH Example

Isabella* had been working in an Adult Family Home in the Seattle, WA area for eight months. The commute was long and costly, as she used Uber. A friend leaving a caregiver job referred Isabella as her replacement in a home operated by MyAFH. It was a much shorter commute, and soon Isabella realized she was benefitting from this new job in other important ways. Although Isabella had some experience, under the tutelage of Patricia, the AFH operator, she honed her skills in cooking, resident care, documentation, and current policies. In her prior AFH experience she had not received much supervision and was not made aware of how she could improve her performance. She had not been kept current on policy changes and how to stay up to date through communications from DSHS (Department of Social and Health Services, State of Washington).

Through experiences with good supervision at the MyAFH home, Isabella learned the proper way to conduct day-to-day operations of an AFH. She worked diligently over the next year and became confident in her abilities. After working two years as a caregiver, Isabella got an opportunity to advance. Her supervisor Patricia knew that an AFH business was seeking an operator, and recommended Isabella for consideration. Patricia believed Isabella had great potential for a future in this industry, having watched her progress over the years as a caregiver. Isabella was interviewed and selected by MyAFH to become the operator in a home that was already a functioning AFH.

The owner of the home had decided to retire from operating the AFH business, but wanted to keep the real estate. He needed someone else to handle the AFH business and was working with MyAFH to find an operator. It was a perfect match. Isabella took over as the resident manager to manage the caregiving aspects, while waiting for the change of business ownership to complete legal processes through the state. With the help of MyAFH, after this process concluded, Isabella was able to become the operator and business owner of the home.

Isabella benefited significantly from working with an AFH management company. She gained the opportunity to grow her business into a prosperous venture that helped her attain income stability. With this, she will be better able to move forward with her personal goals.

*Each example is real but the actual names have been changed.

Moving Ahead With MyAFH

You are poised at a decision point, having thoroughly examined your path toward launching an AFH business. This chapter has given you the basis for understanding details of operating a senior living facility. The choice now is whether or to launch your business with an experienced team, or to go it alone. Use the checklist below to summarize how ready you are for launching your AFH business. If you need some help, MyAFH wants to be on your team.

YES! I AM READY TO BE AN AFH OWNER/OPERATOR

CHECK BELOW **I HAVE ACCOMPLISHED THESE THINGS FOR MY AFH BUSINESS**

☐ I have the capacity to construct a new or remodel an existing residential facility (TERM).

☐ I have been certified as an operator in the state in which I live.

☐ I am able to hire quality caregivers.

☐ I have a marketing program that ensures that I can fill my beds.

☐ I have systems in place for compliance with all state requirements and inspections.

☐ I have financial accounting systems in place.

☐ I have relationships lined up with suppliers.

7

CONCLUSION

IF YOU'VE MADE it to this juncture in this book, the two above definitions from Webster's dictionary are both directly "in play" as

you arrive at conclusions. You are at the point to conclude the exercise of reading the book, and also poised to reach your personal conclusions about how to engage with the Adult Family Home business. The hope held by

DEF. "con-clu-sion" /kən'klooZHan
Noun
1. the end or finish of an event or process
2. a judgment or decision reached by reasoning

the team at MyAFH is that a thorough enough job has been done of unpacking the essentials of the Adult Family Home realm to provide a way forward for you and your family.

Understanding these essentials is the first step for any individual or family facing the challenge—and the opportunity—of caring for an aging loved one. Choosing to pursue the path of Adult Family Homes is a unique and beneficial pathway forward. The information and guidance provided in this book taps into the solid and proven experiences of seasoned practitioners in the field, from real estate investing to operating AFH businesses to medical care of the elderly.

This forms the cornerstone for making sound decisions concerning your level of involvement with AFHs.

You are now at the point of making your "decision reached by reasoning." It is totally understandable that your family situation is unique, and not every decision, small and large, that goes into a successful AFH venture is clear at this point. However, forward momentum starts with just one small decision. Are you willing to make that first decision?

It may be as small as simply setting the intention to explore your interest in AFHs further by seeking assistance from some competent and considerate experts. The team at MyAFH offers exactly such assistance, with the goal of serving you as you explore further. Their approach is not taking a theoretical way, but from the perspective of your real-world parameters, where your household's "rubber meets the road." This is a multi-faceted process, most likely an unfamiliar one to you, but familiar to the team through years of hands-on experience.

Recap of What You Have Learned

This book has taken you through insights and trends in the senior care industry, drawing from aging population demographics, finances and economics, medicine and health care, investment options, and real estate requirements as these relate to the increasing needs of the elderly. You have also been guided to assess your goals and capabilities and examine which type of senior living and care is best for you and your family. Tools for decision-making have been suggested, and resources available were described, such as using an AFH management company.

Chapter 1 provided an overview and analysis of the senior living and care industry, with statistics emphasizing demographic trends showing rapid rises in the over 65 population and the very old, those over 85, most of whom will need assistance with living. Real-life examples were given of positive and tragic situations faced by families with elderly loved ones. Issues in providing medical care to the elderly were described.

Chapter 2 offered a roadmap through the senior care territory to launch you into your journey. You learned details of the main options in senior care: Assisted Living Facilities, Adult Family Homes, and In Home Care; as well as roles of Nursing Homes and Memory Care. Additional statistics were given for the impact of Baby Boomers reaching age 65, a game-changer in the industry. Examples were provided of costs for these different options.

Chapter 3 examined the ways you can become an investor in Adult Family Homes. People have different motivations and goals for investing, and descriptions of the Real Estate Investor, Social Impact Investor, and Family Steward-Legacy Investor helped you determine where you fit. Examples were given of some investor scenarios and financial information provided for costs and profits. You were able to consider the pros and cons of each approach.

Chapter 4 took you on the next steps once you decided to become involved in an AFH. It provided a model for you to take stock of your Time, Energy, Resources, and Money (TERM) in selecting your level of involvement. Details were given of the three levels of involvement, including real estate owner, AFH operator, and owner/operator, so you could see what would be required. Pros and cons of each level were described, and you were guided to evaluate your TERMs for each. Your basic decision became could you do it alone, or would it be better to team up with an AFH management company.

Chapter 5 guided you through the numerous considerations of whether your property is right for an AFH. Specifics were provided for how to evaluate a property for suitability, whether you are looking at new construction or remodeling an existing home. You were assisted in examining options for working with an AFH management company, including contracting for selected services and paying a management fee, leasing your property to an AFH management company to operate, and forming a partnership with a company to mutually operate the home. Real-life examples of these three approaches, the pros and cons, and financial aspects of each were given.

Chapter 6 took you through the requirements and processes of operating an AFH senior living facility. You learned the legal requirements for certifications and owner/staff trainings for both the facility and care of residents. The importance of many aspects of operations were stressed, including property and grounds, building requirements, caregiving and legal records, supplies and maintenance, oversight and safety. The role of referral agents and benefits of an AFH management company were described. Examples were given of the emerging importance of medical technology and its benefits.

The Import and Impact of Being "On Trend"

In any business endeavor, it is important to follow the trends. Success or failure can depend upon following the trends in relevant markets. Trends will show what people in these markets increasingly need, demand, want, or look for at a particular time and place. Being "on trend" often determines those businesses that become profitable and thrive, and those that lose money and may not survive.

This book has identified some key trends across the markets of Assisted Living Facilities and Adult Family Homes that will be in play for the next 30 years. There are three of these key trends which, if taken advantage of, could result in a thriving business for you and your family across generations: Increased Wealth Transfer, Increased Longevity, and Increased Risk of Pandemics.

Increased Wealth Transfer

Over the next 30 years, there will be more wealth transferred through the Baby Boomers—those now aged 55 to 76—than ever in the history of the world. It is estimated that some *68 trillion dollars* will flow into the hands of Baby Boomers from the previous generation, their parents, and that this money will continue flowing from the Baby Boomers to their children and grandchildren.[1] The impact of this unprecedented wealth transfer, however, will depend on how people handle their money. How much money will be preserved and passed on, and how much will be consumed by unplanned expenses or squandering?

The story of Georgie Best, an outstanding soccer player for Manchester United, illustrates this point. Best had earned millions of pounds over the course of his career, only to end up bankrupt and in debt later. When a BBC reporter asked how this could happen, Best famously explained, "I spent a lot of money on booze, birds (women) and fast cars. The rest I just squandered."[2]

Good family stewards are those who preserve and grow assets and resources they have inherited or been entrusted with managing.

Increased Longevity

Population statistics have amply documented that people are living longer. It is clear that higher percentages of the U.S. population will continue to reach the age of 85+ years. Unfortunately, should current trends persist, half of those who live beyond 85 years will develop some form of dementia. Having dementia requires much higher costs for assisted living in the final years of life. It is not uncommon for a family to burn through an aging parent's assets, which were accumulated over the entire course of their life, in the final three years of that life.

Following trends in Alzheimer's disease and dementia research is key to proactive planning for the final years of life. New approaches to prevention and treatment may reduce the impact of these diseases and keep elders functioning better mentally. Limiting the debilitating effects of dementia will mean lower costs of assisted living care.

Increased Risk of Pandemics

Recent experiences across the globe with the COVID-19 pandemic have starkly revealed what life is like under the shadow of a worldwide health crisis. Of critical importance to trends in the senior care and living industry, the pandemic has exposed the extreme vulnerability of this population. Those elders living in large-scale, institutional assisted living environments have suffered disproportionately with heavy death tolls. Severe measures have been necessary to attempt to control the impact, but it is clear such facilities cannot keep going forward in the same way. Experts warn that conditions are in place for other pandemics in the future.

Adult Family Homes have already shown that they offer a much more controlled, and thereby safer and healthier, eco-system in which to provide care for the elderly. Exposure that leads to the spread of infections is reduced in this small, generally stable setting. This makes Adult Family Homes a very attractive choice for families who want to place loved ones in facilities that can best ensure health and safety. This powerful trend is shaping and will continue to shape the character of the elder care business.

Putting these three trends together, along with their wide-ranging impacts, it becomes clear that there is a great opportunity to be "on trend" in the Adult Family Home business in this particular time and place.

Your Conclusion Regarding Adult Family Homes

In the end, only you can make the decision about launching into the arena of Adult Family Homes. You might be convinced by now that your aging loved one, or yourself, would be best served by spending the last third of life in this type of setting, as opposed to a larger facility or care at home. If that is your decision, but you don't want to engage in the business, you have still benefited from reading this

> "The journey of a thousand miles must begin with a single step."
> —Lao Tzu

book. You've learned a great deal and are better equipped to select and evaluate an AFH for your family. In doing so, your choice leads to an improved living situation on many fronts, considering the choices available today in senior assisted living.

If instead, you conclude that investing in the AFH business, however you choose to be involved and whatever your goals and motives, is the best choice for you rest assured that you will be part of a bright future. The knowledge and insight you gained in this book provide a solid foundation for moving forward. Often it is insight that leads to innovation. Being part of a solution that is both innovative and greatly needed is a rewarding endeavor.

> "The wisdom of the prudent is to give thought to their ways."
> —King Solomon

In addition, if such an endeavor "Does Well (is profitable) while Doing Good (serves others beyond yourself)," then it falls into that category of being a wise investment of one's limited Time, Energy, Resources, and Money. As you consider your and your family's TERMs, there is yet one other conclusion for you to reach: whether to foray into the territory alone or to draw an experienced team to your side.

The team at MyAFH would certainly consider it a worthwhile endeavor on their part to come alongside you and help you further explore the world of Adult Family Homes.

How Can MyAFH Support Your Goals?

Our goal is to change the senior care industry and empower our seniors and their families. For over 15 years, MyAFH has been developing industry partnerships and outlining the process of starting an AFH. With our support, owners will not only save money at the beginning, in addition operating an AFH will bring opportunities and longevity to your business.

Here are some easy ways to connect with the team:

Email: info@AFHSeniorCare.com

Website: http://Afhseniorcare.com

Phone: 800-747-2997

Address: 405 SW 41st Street, Suite 407, Renton, WA 98057

Are you feeling inspired to "design your senior care?" Take a picture of our QR code and get your next steps from AFH Senior Care.

www.afhseniorcare.com/next-steps

GLOSSARY

Adult Family Home (AFH): AFHs are residential homes that have been converted to meet state licensing and requirements for senior housing and care. AFHs have between 1 and 8 residents, and provide meals, housekeeping, and assistance with activities of daily living. (Some states call these Group Homes, Board and Care Homes, or Adult Residential Homes.)

Assisted Living Facilities (ALF): ALFs are state-licensed facilities that provide housing and care to larger numbers of seniors in apartment-style living. Size averages 45 residents to around 200 residents. Housing, meals, and assistance with activities of daily living are provided. Many have amenities such as dining rooms, clubhouses, pools, gyms, and meeting rooms.

(**Note:** Some states do not distinguish between ALFs and AFHs in data keeping.)

AFH Operator: Person or entity that owns the AFH business, or owns both the business and the property. The Operator is the person who oversees the operations of an AFH business. Operators must complete courses required by the state and receive certification.

(In Washington State, Operators are called Providers)

AFH Owner: Used synonymously with AFH Operator. The Operator is always the Owner of an AFH business. However, the Owner of the real estate can be a different person than the Owner of the AFH business.

AFH Investor: Person or entity that invests money into an AFH business or property, or both.

Real Estate Owner: Person or entity that owns the house and property on which an AFH is located. As commonly used, Real Estate Owners generally do not own or operate the AFH business. However, the same person may own both the real estate and the AFH business. In that case they are called Owners and Operators.

AFH Resident Manager: Person who oversees daily care of residents and runs the daily operations of the facility, supervising and training the caregivers in duties and expectations. This is usually a temporary position acting in lieu of the Operator.

AFH Caregiver: Person who provides direct daily care to residents in an AFH. Caregivers must complete courses required by the state and receive certification.

CNA (Certified Nursing Assistant): Person who has completed the CNA coursework and is state-certified. CNAs have skills that would be used in a hospital setting, not tailored to an AFH.

HCA (Home Care Aide): Person who has completed the HCA state certification to work in an AFH. HCAs have skills tailored to the needs of AFH residents.

Continuing Care Retirement Communities (CCRC): A tiered senior residential facility that offers "aging in place" by providing all levels of senior care. Also called life plan communities, all types of care from independent living to assisted living and memory care are housed in the same campus. Residents must buy into the community, and these are very costly.

Independent Senior Living (55+ Communities): Retirement developments for seniors that range from privately owned single residences to condominiums or apartments that are rented. Seniors generally function independently, though third-party care providers can be hired for in-home assistance.

In-Home Care: Families provide care for elders themselves or hire local caregivers for varying daily hours and services. This is still the most widely used option for senior care. As seniors become oldest-old, care needs may be greater or more costly than can be managed in the home setting.

Skilled Nursing Facilities (SNF): SNF's provide medical and nursing professional care to patients making a transition from an acute care hospital to another facility or back home. Services include rehabilitation and skilled services for recovery from strokes, surgery, or acute illness, which generally cannot be managed in assisted living facilities. Length of stay is limited to 120 days by Medicare and most insurance.

(**Note:** SNFs are not long-term care options. However, many ALFs have mixed beds for both skilled nursing care and long-term care).

Nursing Home: An older term for long-term care facilities. In common usage the term includes almost all facilities for residential care of elderly or disabled people. Nursing homes are also referred to as Assisted Living Facilities, Skilled Nursing Facilities, old people's homes, care homes, rest homes, and convalescent care homes. Adult Family Homes are usually not included in the nursing home category.

Health: A state of complete physical, mental and social wellbeing and not merely the absence of disease or infirmity. (World Health Organization)

Healthcare: Actions or endeavors made to support the promotion or restoration of health.

Healthcare delivery: The actions of promotion of health by people, institutions, and material and non-material resources.

Healthcare services: All of the institutions, processes, logistics supporting medicine, public health, healthcare delivery

Clinical medicine: The delivery of and provision of medicine by licensed professionals.

Medicine: The concepts and implementation of the materials, study, science, and practice of supporting healthcare.

Public health: The art and science of preventing disease, prolonging life, and promoting health through the organized efforts of society. (World Health Organization)

ABOUT THE AUTHORS

Christian Potra brings over 20 years of experience and innovation to the Adult Family Home model of elder care. The systems, processes, training, and attention to personal needs and requirements of residents under his care are what have propelled the growth of 16+ homes in the Seattle Metro area. Chris' enthusiasm for bringing this alternative to the traditional institutional model of assisted living to a wider market is the driving force behind this book.

Stephen Morris, MD, MPH, started his professional career in education, ecology, and international development before moving onto medicine, always with the intention of combining it with public health. His clinical specialty is Emergency Medicine, and holds the position of Assistant Professor of Emergency Medicine and an Adjunct Assistant Professor of Global Health at the University of Washington's Schools of Medicine and Public Health, respectively.

Michael Hearl has teamed up with Christian for the past five years in building the marketing and financial cornerstones of the Adult Family Home business, bringing his experience in both the ministry and real estate development worlds. Michael is intent upon working alongside families who carry a keen sense of the importance of being good stewards of family resources while providing the best possible care for loved ones.

ENDNOTES

INTRODUCTION

1. Administration for Community Living, U.S. Department of Health and Human Services. U.S. Census Bureau, National Center for Health Statistics. Profile of Older Americans, 2017-2018. Washington, DC.

2. Kate Brown Wilson. "Historical Evolution of Assisted Living in the Unites States, 1979 to The Present." *The Gerontologist*, Vol. 47, Special Issue III. The Gerontological Society of America, 2007.

3. David Hochman. "An American Tragedy: Covid-19 and Nursing Homes." Special Edition Nursing Homes, *AARP Bulletin,* Vol. 61, No. 10, December 2020. AARP, Washington, DC.

4. Harris Meyer. "A Failing Business Model: Covid-19 has revealed—and worsened—weaknesses in nursing home finances." Special Edition Nursing Homes, *AARP Bulletin,* Vol. 61, No. 10, December 2020. AARP, Washington, DC.

1 GETTING THE LAY OF THE LAND

1. The Baby Boomer Generation. Senior Living, March 13, 2020. www.seniorliving.org /life/baby-boomers. Accessed online November 2020.

2. 2019 Profile of Older Americans, U.S. Department of Health and Human Services, Administration for Community Living. Principal data sources: U.S. Census Bureau, National Center for Health Statistics, Bureau of Labor Statistics. www.acl.gov

3. "Nursing Homes Must Test for Covid-19." *AARP.ORG Bulletin*, October 2020, Vol. 61, No. 8. Based on data from the Centers for Medicare & Medicaid Services.

4. 2019 Profile of Older Americans, U.S. Department of Health and Human Services, Administration for Community Living. Principal data sources: U.S. Census Bureau, National Center for Health Statistics, Bureau of Labor Statistics. www.acl.gov

5. Paying for Senior Care: Understand Your Financial Options for Long-Term Care. "What is Home Health Care and How Much Does It Cost?" www.payingforseniorcare.com, accessed 10/18/20.

6. AHCA/NCAL – American Health Care Association/National Center for Assisted Living. https://www.ahcancal.org/Data-and-Research/Pages. Accessed 10/17/20.

7. Assisted Living In Washington. Senior Homes.com. www.seniorhomes.com /washington. Accessed online October 2020.

8. David Mancuso, "Estimating Nursing-Home-Comparable Home and Community-Based Service Capacity," DSHS Research and Data Analysis Division, RDA Report 8.35, Olympia, Washington.

9. "Dementia," Cleveland Clinic, July 16, 2020. www.my.clevelandclinic.org/health /diseases/9170-dementia, accessed 10/17/20.

10. Senior Homes, www.seniorhomes.com, accessed 10/14/20; Senior Care, www. seniorcare.com, accessed 10/14/20.

11. Adult Family Home Council (AFHC) of Washington State, www.adultfamily homecouncil.org, accessed 6/26/20.

2 DESIGNING YOUR MAP THROUGH
THE SENIOR CARE TERRITORY

1. Based on U.S. Census Bureau, National Center for Health Statistics (2017-2018), NIH National Research Council, National Institute on Aging. Accessed online Oct-Dec 2020.

2. *Profile of Older Americans 2017*, U.S. Census Bureau, National Center for Health Statistics, and Bureau of Labor Statistics, 2018. (p2)

3. U.S. Department of Health and Human Services (DHHS),The Administration for Community Living-Administration on Aging, 2018. (p2)

4. Linda Breytspraak. "How Many Seniors Really End Up In Nursing Homes?" Center on Aging Studies, University of Missouri-Kansas City. Posted online January 6, 2016. (p2)

5. Joe Eaton. "Reimagining the Nursing Home: After COVID-19, here's what experts say may change." AARP Bulletin, Your Health, June 2020. (p3,7)

6. James Berris. "Employee Turnover in Senior Care." Senior Care Staff Turnover By The Numbers & Why It Matters To You. www.onshift.com/blog/senior-care-staff-turnover. Accessed online November 2020.

7. "An American Tragedy: Covid-19 and Nursing Homes." Special Edition Cover Story, *AARP Bulletin, Vol. 61 No. 10,* December 2020. AARP, Washington, DC.

8. Kate Brown Wilson. "Historical Evolution of Assisted Living in the United States, 1979 to The Present." *The Gerontologist*, Vol. 47, Special Issue III. The Gerontological Society of America, 2007.

9. Ronald L. Moore. "The Basics of Assisted Living," FamilyCare America, Inc., 2019. www.caregiverslibrary.org/Caregivers-Resources, accessed online July, 2020. (p8)

10. Medicare & You, 2021. The Official U.S. Government Medicare Handbook. Part A Hospital Insurance, pp 25-29. Centers for Medicare and Medicaid Services, Department of Health and Human Services, 2020. (p9 x2)

11. NIC Investment Guide: Investing in Seniors Housing & Care Properties, Fifth Edition. National Investment Center, 2018. www.nic.org. (p9)

12. Jeff Hoyt, Editor in Chief, Senior Living.Org. Personal Care Homes, August 2018. SeniorLiving.org, accessed online October, 2020. (p12)

13. About Adult Family Homes. Adult Family Home Council of Washington State. www.adultfamilyhomecouncil.org/about-us, accessed online June, 2020. (p13)

3 AFH INVESTOR SCENARIOS

1. NIC Investment Guide – National Investment Center for Seniors Housing & Care Properties, Fifth Edition, 2018.

2. John Mackey and Raj Sisoda. *Conscious Capitalism.* Harvard Business School Publishing Corporation, Boston, Massachusetts, 2014.

3. Elder Abuse Facts. National Council on Aging. www.ncoa.org/public-policy-action/elder-abuse. Accessed online November, 2020.

4 DO I HAVE WHAT IT TAKES?

1. John Naisbitt. *Megatrends: Ten New Directions Transforming Our Lives*. Grand Central Publishing, Division of Hatchette Book Group, NY (1988)

5 IS MY PROPERTY RIGHT FOR AN AFH?

1. AFH Management Acquisition Package. MyAFH, Renton, WA 2019.

6 OPERATING A SENIOR LIVING FACILITY

1. 75-Hour Training and Home Care Aide Certification Overview (Revised September, 2019). Department of Social and Health Services (DSHS), Washington State, Olympia, WA. www.dshs.wa.gov. Accessed online November 2020.

2. Training Requirements Summary for Adult Family Homes. Washington State Department of Social and Health Services (DSHS). Aging and Long-Term Support Administration (ALTSA). https://www.dshs.wa.gov/altsa/training/training-reuirements -adult-family-homes. Accessed online September, 2020.

3. Washington State Legislature, Elder and Vulnerable Adult Referral Agency Act. RWC (Revised Code of Washington) Title 18, Chapter 18.330.010 Definitions, https://app.leg. wa.gov/rcw. Accessed online November 2020.

4. Most Frequently Cited Adult Family Homes Regulations. Data Source: FAC1008 _CitationsAfhBhState. Report Parameters: 1/1/2016 to 3/31/2016. Accessed online February 2017.

7 CONCLUSION

1. Andrew Osterland. "What the coming $68 trillion Great Wealth Transfer means for financial advisors." Financial Advisor 101, CNBC, Oct. 21, 2019. https://www.cnbc. com/2019/10/21/what-the-68-trillion-great-wealth-transfer-means-for-advisors.html. Accessed online December 2020.

2. "Best: Decline of the golden boy." news.bbc.co.uk. June 14, 2005. https://www. azquotes.com/quote/25925. Accessed online December 2020.